# MEN LOVE WOMEN .........WOMEN LOVE THEMSELVES

## *Fact or Fallacy?*

# P "NALAGY" BROWNE

## BROWNWISE
*Reaching Tomorrow Today*

Published by BROWNWISE PUBLISHING

For information, please go to www.brownwisepublishing.com

ISBN 13: 978-0-578-06285-3

LCCN: 2010912690

Printed in the United States of America

# DEDICATION

*Dedicated to my parents: Genevieve and Charlesworth - both of whom I love dearly. It is my firm belief that if the information within the pages of this Book was available to you, at the opportune time, it would have aided you in saving your blissful relationship and marriage.*

# ACKNOWLEDGEMENTS

There are so many people to thank and acknowledge for making this Book a reality, I don't know exactly where to start. However, I'll do my endeavor best to include everyone.

First and foremost, I want to thank my immediate family for all their continued love and support during the writing of this book. Also, I want to extend a special a "thank you" to my brothers, Michael and Mc Lean, and to my nephew, Sean for sharing their thoughts and providing encouragement at times when I needed it most.

Secondly, I want to extend special acknowledgements to Susan and Stephanie, who were two major sources of inspiration in turning this dream into a reality for me. Thanks for everything!

Thirdly, I want to extend special thanks to Craig for his initial feedback and heartfelt motivational words which led to the kick-off and relentless pursuit and ultimate completion of this project.

Next, I want to acknowledge those who (knowingly or unknowingly) helped me with my research and perspective throughout this book: Andrew, Deepak, Prudence, Don, Craig, Yaseen, Ralphus, Debbie, Carisa, Latha, Michelle, Karron, Erica, Mony, Martin, Mc Lean, Michael, Craig, and all others – too numerous to mention.

Also, I want to thank all the men and women who participated in the interviewing process: Thanks for all your time and sincerity; I truly appreciated your varied inputs.

Last, but not least, I want to thank all the divinely orchestrated coincidences – in time and space – which mysteriously presented themselves, precisely when needed, to actively impart the necessary inspiration and insight required to push me to the next level in my writing. Thank you very, very much!


Thank You All!

# TABLE OF CONTENTS

| Chapter | Page |
|---|---|

# INTRODUCTION

I am quite aware of the fact that my choice for the title of this book: *"Men Love Women…Women Love Themselves" is* bound to provoke some immediate emotional reactions in the way of being seemingly offensive to some. I personally think this would be a good thing, though: perplexity occasionally encourages thought, and thought often piques curiosity. For example, upon sharing the title of this book with a friend, who happens to be a woman, her immediate response was,

"You have a problem with women…..don't you?"

I do understand, clearly, that the typical egotistical mind would very likely be slighted or even vehemently offended by the initial assertion of this title. However, my *"Fact or Fallacy"* subtitle specifically serves as a sort of *cushion* - if you will - which should or would, hopefully, lead to some level of personal approval or disapproval of my declaration, after thoroughly examining my embarked-upon approach and perspective on the issue.

Have you ever noticed how much some of us seem to always be on the alert to be offended or *"pissed-off"* – in some way or another – by something or someone else? We approach life as if everyone we encounter - on the road, in the supermarket, at work, in the store, at the airport, in the bank, at Church, at the Post Office, on the television; and especially so, those who attempt to share any advice which conflicts with our ingrained belief systems - has a mission in that space and time to deliberately *upset* or *annoy* us to some degree. So that you'd know, if that is the way you normally react to life, you are indeed controlled by your ever-present, weakening, always dissatisfied, and forever-ready-to-be-offended Ego or *Lower Self!* If this is so, being upset or "pissed-off" at others would very likely be your general, everyday, habituated way of being.

On the other hand, your *Upper Self* or that part of your psyche driven and directed by Universal Intelligent *Knowing, knows* that we as humans are all connected - spiritually; *knows* that no one offends anyone else without their *inner* approval to be offended; *knows* that every experience we encounter in life is designed to teach us *something else* about ourselves; *knows* that every book, billboard, song on the radio, letter in the mail box, or anything else that captures our attention is, without question, something we *attracted* or, more precisely, "sent-for" as a result of the dominant thoughts we've been harboring in that particular time and space. For example, your present dominant thoughts may be centered on why your relationships don't ever seem to *work out*.....and *lo and behold,* you just attracted this book to you to show you why! Isn't that *GREAT?*

Know that everything happens in precise divine order. This simply means there are *no accidents* or *coincidences* in life. Know this! You can only benefit from this "Knowing" by your participation or grasp of what it really means. Remember, it's affecting you whether you decide to accept it as truth or not!

This book is designed to provoke personal insightful awareness. It is my fervent belief that too many of us are walking around with our *eyes wide shut* to the simplest of truths to life. Further, this book is slotted to encourage examination of the many *causes* behind the resulting *effects* we refer to as our reality - both in our relationships and in our entire lives as a whole. Remember: our relationships are *not* separate from the rest of our lives! We're always living the *effects* - if you will - of the decisions, actions and/or inner thought-patterns *(causes)* we either continually uphold, or have upheld in the past, resulting in the conditions or circumstances we are facing *in the now.* Charles F Haanel in his book titled, *The Master Key System,* wrote the following in reference to this same reality to life. He wrote:

"The ordinary man, who has no definite knowledge of *cause* and *effect,* is governed by his feelings or emotions. He thinks chiefly to justify his actions. If he fails as a businessman, he says that his luck is against him. If he dislikes music, he says that music is an expensive luxury. If he is a poor office man, he says he could succeed better at some outdoor work. If he lacks friends, he says his individuality is *too fine* to be appreciated. He never thinks his problem through to the end. In short, he does not know that every *effect* (he faces) is the result of a certain definite *cause*, but (instead) he seeks to console himself with *explanations* and *excuses*. He thinks only in *self-defense...*"

Even though my discussion in this book will be centered specifically on personal relationships, it is a fact that *all of life encompasses relationships*. It's *a truth* we simply cannot escape! This means that every relationship - your relationship with your spouse, your relationship with your Boss, your relationship with your neighbors, your relationship with the supermarket or Post Office attendant, your relationship with your parents, your relationship with your kids, your relationship with the person sharing the road with you, your relationship with the person you encountered in the parking lot, etc - in some way or another, affects every other. For example, do you really think the person who clandestinely jumps in-front of you in line at the Bank, or the person who boldly takes the parking spot he or she knew - quite well - you were diligently waiting for, genuinely cares about other people's feelings - including the other person or persons in his or her personal relationship(s)? Think again!

However, deep inside the premise: "all of life encompasses relationships," there is this one fundamental reality that most of us somehow fail to come to grips with: *Our most important relationship is the kind of relationship we conduct with ourselves!* If your relationship with yourself is *not* one driven-by and filled-with self-love and self-respect, then it's an absolute impossibility for you to love and respect anyone else - no matter how hard you may try!

Of course, the opposite is also true: once you truly love and respect yourself, you'll naturally love and respect everyone else. Yes, this is not a typo, I did mean *everyone else!* It means that your relationship with yourself is and should be of utmost importance to you, and will - without question - directly impact, positively or negatively, all of your life-long experiences. Our ability to grasp *this one reality* to life - in my mind - will unequivocally serve as the unmistakable, underlying solution to each and every *known* relationship problem we face. Remember, everything *begins* and *ends* with loving the *Self!*

Ok, let's get down to the *"nitty-gritty"* of things. I am sure the one question that keeps sticking out in your mind is that you'd really like to know why I chose such an assertion as *"Men Love Women......Women Love Themselves!"* for the topic of this book? I know my initial discussion on *perplexity* never really answered this question; therefore, I'll do my best here to divulge the reasoning for my choice.

Initially, upon deciding to embark on this project, I frankly didn't have any idea what title I was going to use – none! Of course, I've had my own experiences in life, and I do carry my own personal viewpoints on relationships, etc; but nonetheless, I decided to move forward with an unbiased, open mind as much as possible. My path forward was to conduct my research from the premise of just simply *Allowing* the men and women I interviewed to freely vent their concerns with little or no direction or interference from myself.

As I went ahead, interviewing and conducting these in-depth relationship-based discussions with men from different *walks of life* - including, but not limited to, immediate and distant family members: some married; some about to be married; and still others, having no intention whatsoever to ever be married - it became clearer and clearer to me that, collectively, there seem to be *one underlying tone* imbedded in just about every concern vented to me by these men. And that is, the majority felt extremely *unloved*, and correspondingly *disempowered* in their relationships. They felt as if they've been *'loving'* their women (especially so the married ones) all along, while they've (their wives, etc) been busy *'loving'* themselves! Bingo!

Don't get me wrong, none of the men came out and verbally coined those words; it was what they were *"not saying"* that I eventually picked-up on. The undertone of the majority was an almost deafening scream of: *"I LOVE HER, BUT SHE ONLY LOVES HERSELF!"*

Of course, this could very well be a subconscious misconception on the side of the men.....thus the reason for this Book, and the further reason for my choice of subtitle: "*Fact or Fallacy?*" The Reader will be given the opportunity to decide if there is indeed any truth to my declaration. And please remember, I am only *The Messenger*!

How exactly are relationships viewed or defined in our society? All of the following are considered to be normal: The man provides.....the woman receives. The man provides "security"....the woman receives "security" – whether it's by physical protection, material comfort, or otherwise. During courtship, the man is *expected* to pay for all forms of entertainment.....the woman is committed mostly to how well entertained she can possibly be by the particular man. When a woman meets a man, he's viewed as "A Good Catch" if he has a significantly large income, and is "living well" – in her mind. For most, his personality and level of - or lack of - loyalty is not remotely considered when arriving at this premature conclusion. Most men, on the other hand, consider a woman to be "A Good Catch" solely based on her *looks*. Are most men superficial? Are most women *Gold Diggers*? Let's find out.

Are most men superficial? Not necessarily. I am a man, and I'll say, at first, a woman's *looks* are very, very, important to me in the way of her physical attraction. However, although her *looks* initially attracts me, it's her personality, sex-appeal, and corresponding depth of character - in terms of her *in-sync-with-my-own* fundamentals - that will eventually lead to any possibility of a meaningful relationship with me. In other words, her outward beauty or "looks" does not *remotely* make her into "A Good Catch" for me.

Are most women *Gold Diggers*? I'll say it's all dependent on your viewpoint of what "Gold Diggers" are? In my opinion, a "Gold Digger" is any woman (or man) who makes conscious effort to eagerly and deliberately orchestrate the opportunity to be with a man (or woman) *solely based on his or her status* as it relates to fame (as in popularity), income, occupation, or influence. The main driver here is that it typically hovers around the notion of "What do I stand to gain, materially, from this person." I am not here to point anyone out……..you know who you are!

I have come to realize that there are millions of men in our society today, who are in bitter resentment for the Institution of Marriage; and mainly because, they took it upon themselves, sometime earlier in life, to marry a "look-good" type woman, who turned-out to be absolutely "no-good" for them – in their minds. Typically, after their so-called *blissful* union, marriage, the man soon come to realize there was *absolutely nothing* about the particular woman's personality, inner beauty, or otherwise, that remotely measured-up to the external *Illusion of Beauty* which got him *hooked* in the first place.

Faced with this foregoing dilemma, what do most men do to correct or rectify the situation? Typically *nothing!* They would give-up all possibilities for happiness, in a seemingly unselfish way, to stay in these *state of affairs*, voluntarily indoctrinate themselves along with the other "It's Cheaper To Keep Her" millions, who retire to live the rest of their lives in utter despair and discontentment.

Often, men appear to be natural protectors and nurturers of women; so - to most - a part of all this may seem rather normal. However, what's not normal is the fact that most of these same women would sometimes be constantly scheming to change these men into what appear to be their "Little Projects." Typically, once the particular "Project" is completed, some would naturally desire another "Project" to work-on or change. Commonly, when and if this "Project" completion takes place, the only factor that manages to keep the typical woman in the particular relationship, or marriage, is the "Security Factor" - if and only if it exists! This is the point where the typical woman intensifies the act of *running* the relationship, through the common practice of *sexual-rationing*. This situation in turn, leaves the particular man no choice, according to some, but to "step-out."   ,

Remember, the husband was "A Good Catch," so the particular woman may be a stay-at-home mom or wife enjoying the fruits of *"The Catch,"* and, at the same time, making his life a *living hell!*

Often, she'll probably stay with him because of the seeming, naturally-occurring, self-centered, selfish nature that some women have voluntarily bought-into and adapted as their own. All this would sometimes seem normal since, in the typical woman's mind, men are like puppets: "They have no true feelings; they have no true emotions or compassion about them; they need to be *controlled* and *directed,* in order to *give us what we must have,* since it's all about us - anyways!"

Sadly, the man's needs and desires are always secondary to hers. If they happen to conflict – ever – his would usually be mentally dismissed as being unimportant! In other words, his needs only seem to become important if they are in-keeping with hers!

Further, I have concluded that what a woman refers to as "love for a man," is commonly based solely on *how he makes her feel.* Conversely, I have also found that what a man refers to as "love for a woman," is generally based, partially, on how he believes he *makes* her feel, or her overall reaction towards him, coupled with a logical decision to love and accept her for *who she is, as she is*; the latter being driven entirely by societal expectations of him.

Therefore, as is obvious, a man's love seems to be based-on *feed-back* from the particular woman (unselfish); whereas, a woman's love seems to be based on the way the particular man *makes* her feel. The man, being an external entity, remains valuable as long as he is able to continue to induce these feelings inside her (selfish). This is the reason why, outside of the so-called "Security Factor," if another man is able to make any woman "feel better" or "happier" - as some would say - than her present *man* or husband (even if he may show clear signs of possibly being abusive), he can technically and absolutely "have her" – without question! It seems to be *all about feelings* for the typical woman.

On the issue of *marriage* and its forerunner, *commitment,* I will put aside their dictionary meanings here; I will instead, focus on what these terms collectively mean in practicing reality.

Initially, I was prompted to confine this piece to western societies; but today, as it stands, the social and cultural practices in western societies –

especially so that of the USA – seem to unfortunately be effectively acting as the *gauge* for the rest of the inhabited World, as we know it. The US culture, being a direct by-product of European Colonialism, has been viciously immersed in European customs and practices; this leading to the many "false values" and "false truths" - in my opinion - which we readily embrace and act-upon as *our inescapable reality*. For example, we can't seem to understand why marriages simply don't work; and why approximately 90% of the ones that seem to work, have effectively failed since their early years. Nonetheless, many married couples have chosen to stay together "for the sake of the kids," as some would say; or sometimes, because of the unwarranted, debilitating *fear of being alone*.

I have concluded that our beliefs always govern our actions; therefore, if we continue to believe the same old out-dated things, we're doomed to act and interact in the same old ways, which can only lead to the same old undesirable results. Consequently, although we keep-on banging our heads against the *iron walls of life,* most insist on fiercely continuing down the same path – generation after generation. We can't seem to understand that *change* begins from *within*; we instead, keep clinging to the belief system which says: "if any *change* is going to come......it's going to come from *out there - somewhere!*" Change what you believe by tapping into your *inner knowing,* and you'll be amazed how soon your circumstances change – all for the better!

Also, come to grips with the fact that you *cannot* make your husband or wife change! You *can* only provide encouragement which would hopefully generate some level of change in them. Nevertheless, you cannot *make* anyone else *do anything*! In actuality, you can only *change yourself* by changing what you *choose to believe* and act upon. If this is so-so difficult for most of us to accomplish, imagine the impossible task it must entail in attempting to change someone else.

"I've loved you all my life....though you've been busy loving only yourself...." or so you thought! "If I don't love myself...who's going to love me?" You would say - not realizing that rightfully loving yourself does not exclude or negate the other person in your life.

I have coined the true essence of *Love* to mean, *The Unselfish Respect* and *Appreciation One Holds for One's Own Existence*. This – in my mind – is the true *aura of love*, which draws all others to us naturally.

*Unselfish*, because you cannot guard it or possess it; you must give it away freely - like the Heavens gives us rain, the sun gives us sunlight, and the moon gives us moonlight. The more you give of it....the more it returns – ten-folds! Therefore, you can't *keep it* and *have it* all at the same time. Try to keep it, for yourself, and it's the sure way to lose it all. For it to remain, you can only be a witness to it and unselfishly bask in its aura.

*Respect*, because being *Unselfish* naturally leads to self-respect, which is another cornerstone that exists definitively in the *aura of love*. You cannot give *Respect* unless you have it within you and subsequently about you to give. And it's not like saying, "Ok, here you have it!" It's more like, whatever you're filled with *within*, will naturally and noticeably emit *without* and *about you*.

And *Appreciation*, since as long as you're in a constant state of *Unselfish Respect* for Self, deep *Gratitude* or a prevailing sense of *positive reception* for all of life – within and without – becomes your naturally-occurring state of being.

In my mind, these three characteristics constitutes the many facets of the phenomenon we call *LOVE*.

May this book fulfill my intention to provide each and every reader with only the necessary insight specific to his or her particular needs. And further, may this work serve as the divinely-inspired *spark* which will initiate, encourage, and ultimately lead to more harmonious relationships in our society and every other society throughout our inhabited World. *I am certain* that anything and everything is *indeed* possible.

P "Nalagy" Browne
5-7-2009

# CHAPTER 1

## The Making of the "Dogg"

He waggles his tail, and yawns with selfish gratification, as he retreats from his latest sexual encounter. Now considered a past object of pursuit, disguised by false claims of love and life-long desire, the Dogg's only true objective is to seek-out and conquer his next victim, which could very well be any woman: your sister, your best friend, your next door neighbor; and just about any other woman or girl he considers to be sexually desirable - while, at the same time, keeping you *hanging-on* to his false hope of commitment. He operates like this, simply because - like the true dog, *man's best friend* - it's in his nature to be that way.

Sadly, this is the prevailing viewpoint of many young women in our society today - ages 25 and above - when it comes to men and what they consider as being men's primary objective in relationships; thus the term, "Men Are Doggs" was born. This thought pattern, seems to be one of the fundamental reasons why women are so adamant about commitment (marriage) from about age 30, onwards. In their minds, if they can somehow keep this *"Dogg"* on a *short leash* (marriage), he would be deterred from committing such promiscuous acts. And if he does, he would be faced with deep-rooted consequences - including, but not limited to, a notorious *dent* in his finances.

However, even though we cannot refute the fact that there might be some level of truth to this dogma, depending on the particular viewpoint held, most "Doggs" were never born....they were created!

Remember when you were at about age sixteen.........your body started blooming and you begun feeling those new womanly changes occurring inside your body and mind? You began filling-out those jeans;

and *suddenly,* all men gave you *double takes* whenever you pass by. Soon, you began craving this new-found attention, so you became more and more concerned with your outward appearance: what you're wearing, your hair, your skin; and today, even the desire to put-on make-up, etc. To your surprise and amazement, this one guy at school or at the local park, who you had the "BIG CRUSH" on, as a kid, and up until a year ago didn't even acknowledge you were even *alive,* is now 'sweating you' like a *steam room.*

Crazy but true, this marks one of the birthplaces of the ever-growing female ego, or, for lack of a better term, the female obsession with herself; her self-importance – if you will. I am not sure if it's the naturally-occurring changes in her hormones, or the natural growth of her deep-rooted ego, but from this point onwards, the guys with the *lifelong affection eyes* better watch-out: *Attention* now becomes her purpose, and what she *thinks* she *must have* now becomes her God.

Strangely enough, all these changes will more often than not be entirely based on feelings sparked and, for the most part, induced by external forces acting as the trigger. With most women, it seems as if logical mental decision-making, when it comes to men, is only sorted out and practiced later on in life when the *Dogg Pact* has already been created, and experience has proven that something internal *must* be changed or adjusted in order to find men who would remotely take them seriously. And even then, the prevailing "How I Am Feeling Right Now" decision-making-forces still remain ever so dominant.

I want to make it resoundingly clear here that this piece is not intended to offend anyone. It is merely to recognize that even though we may be simply doing what seems natural to us, we could, at the same time, be affecting fundamental changes in the viewpoints of ourselves (as a gender) to others. And although there are no right or wrong answers, if the women and men in our society were to make concerted effort to try and accept each other, without contingencies, and were to further come to the realization that we must always *strive to be what we expect* from that other person in our life, relationships today might finally stand a fighting chance to not only *survive*, but to *thrive*.

Back to our scenario: Often, some unsuspecting young man would probably meet and start dating this *suddenly-feeling-beautiful* young woman - boosting her confidence more and more. Chances are she'll stay with him for as long as he is able to keep her *feeling good*. Feeling-good to the extent that when she's with him she feels *happy;* he makes her smile, laugh, and generally induce feelings of well-being within her. For her, this would be all fun, fun, fun at this time; she'll probably swear, and claim with deep conviction, how much she is *head- over-heels* in love with him then.

What's sad here is that men's feelings for women seem to develop by what I referred to earlier as a *feedback process*. This means that a man develops affection and - what we call - *Love* for a woman based on her reactions towards him in every sense of the word. Remember, he makes her *feel good*.......she's happy; she now wants to see him every *dying moment*; to spend time with him; to hang-out with him; to make-out with him, etc. Here, as a young man, chances are he'd be *naturally* falling for her. So, commonly, at such point it is very likely that both parties would be absolutely certain that they're so much in-love with each other.

Further, in the typical guys mind, falling-in-love with this girl is indeed the logical thing to do and be. He would probably be thinking some version of, "If I am responsible for her feeling *this way* about me, then she must be *The One* for me, since she makes me feel like a KING also." Being the logical gender, at such tender age (15 or 16), guys usually cling to these beliefs, deeply convincing themselves that they'll both feel this way for the rest of their lives.

As it stands, this relationship may last for a short while; probably a few months or so. However, more often than not, with the natural cycle of emotions in young women, and with these natural hormonal changes being relatively new, at this delicate time, one of two things usually transpire.

First, when things are new, emotions are commonly overshadowed. Thus, after a few weeks, the *newness* may somewhat die-off. Here, it is rather common for the typical girl to just, out-of -the-blue, break-up with the typical guy for no logical reason that he can make any sense of. This act usually devastates the guy, since, in his mind, it doesn't make logical sense that just yesterday it seemed as if she couldn't survive without him in her life, and now - today - she wants out!

Being a personal victim of such situation at the tender age of 16, I can't emphasize enough the deep emotional pain that something of this *magnitude* can cause. I used the word "magnitude" here because an event like this can be life-changing for the relatively young male. In his mind, what makes sense is the fact that she falsely led him-on by pretending to love and care for him. What's worse is he fell for her and for the lie! Here, the average guy would more often than not believe in his heart that her real, purposeful, intentions were solely to hurt him.

Just imagine, a young man now realizing at such tender age, through logical deduction, that the action of a young woman - *The World's most desirable creature to him* - feels like that of an enemy! This, I believe, can and has resulted in deep-rooted resentment on both a conscious and subconscious level; and not only for that particular girl in question, but possibly for the entire gender as a whole! Can he truly trust another woman with his feelings? Should he?

Conversely, in the girls mind, this is not "feeling good" to her as before, so why stick around? To give some understanding to her seeming abrupt decision, we need to shed light on the fact that since she operates mostly on emotions at this stage of her life - typically, can we blame her for acting on how she's feeling at the time, when it seems completely normal to her? For example, consider chocolate and women's love for it. Most would tell you they eat chocolate because it tastes good. We now know the real reason is simply because chocolate actually makes them *feel good*. This is why when some women are depressed they turn to chocolate products for refuge. It's all about "feeling good!" And, once again, logical decision-making takes the proverbial back seat.

Second, sometimes early in the so-called "feel-good" period of the relationship, another guy - a little older or maybe a little more experienced than the first - may give this young woman some attention she could not ignore. Usually, when older guys give younger girls "the time of day" - so to speak - they get all smitten; and especially so, if he's a jock or a popular figure in school or at some equivalent high-contact social setting. Being seen on the arms of such a guy is a *sure-shot* way to gain *instant popularity* with *bragging rights* and 'points' to match. With this *popularity bug* nudging at her, chances are the first guy would be the last to know *it was over* between them.

Most times, though, the situation unfolds with the victim being faced with brutal humiliation from both friends and peers alike. But, to her, even though she may - at this time - still "feel good" with and about the first guy, she now convinces herself that she *should* feel even better with and about the older, more mature guy; the one who every other girl supposedly dieing to be with. In this type ego-boosting situation, considering the extent of hurt and humiliation caused to the other party will be the farthest thing from her mind. To her, the cost of gaining the advantage is insignificant, so "he should just get-over it, and simply.. move-on!"

Often, some types would even go a bit further by continuing to see both guys; giving much priority to the second guy. Without question, it would clearly be a hopeless situation for the younger, seemingly less mature, guy.

If you are a guy and you haven't personally experienced this, try to imagine a young man in a High School setting, for example. This is the place where he's compelled to spend most of the day for at least five days a week. I can't think of any greater torture! In situations like this, some guys may undergo extreme withdrawal symptoms, ranging from severe depression, to *'cutting'* classes; and sometimes, may even resort to abandoning school - altogether. Some may even go as far as despising women to the point of not ever wanting to be in another male-female relationship for the rest of their lives. The latter may seem a bit extreme to some of us.....but as the saying goes, "Who feels it knows it." We need to grasp that it *CAN* get this *DEEP!!*

Of course, there are some guys who are more resilient; and so, are able to shake-off the shame and disappointment rather quickly, and move-on.

I sincerely believe that the time in our lives most of us refer to as "The infatuation period" (between the ages of approx. 12 to 16), is actually the time when we really do feel and exhibit unconditionally true Love for others. Let me explain from a male point of view, since I happen to be one. It is probably the only time when our feelings of Love for that special person is genuinely pure and uncontrived, and not overshadowed by profession, comparative beauty, his or her type car, his or her family's money, or any of the other factors which completely influence our choices of partners later-on in life. I also believe the reason why some of us keep feeling as if we can't seem to ever find the so-called "right person" to make us feel complete and loved, in an adequate way, may more often than not stem from us continually attempting to recapture those genuine feelings we experienced in the so-called 'infatuation period' of our lives.

Let's now fast-forward from ages 16 to 18, all the way to ages 25 to 30. By this time, some guys have already undergone 2 to 3 episodes of hurt and disappointment – long before age 20. The guys who have had such experiences, for the most part, already concluded, mentally, that after picking-up the pieces from their initial emotional hurt and tried again - not once, but twice or more - with equivalent results, are now absolutely convinced that giving and sharing their love and emotions with the opposite sex is definitely not in their best interest. This would be more of an outward act, based-on or caused by the mental or subconscious inner *conditioning,* developed as a result of the adverse, deep-rooted experiences they faced - all at the hands of the opposite sex.

This usually marks the point where these boys, who have now become men, begin to realize that the answer to "protecting themselves" from the familiar *pain* they now conclude to be an integral part of relationships, is to "play the part," rather than actually involving their love and emotions in it.

Here, it is useful to realize that consciously and thus subconsciously also, men seem to be more logical beings. It follows that after years of going through the same pains, their minds go into what I like to call, *Emotional Protect Mode.* Put simply, our minds are designed by nature to protect our emotions; and so, since men (and women) in some ways or another possess an integral need or natural desire to be intimately involved with each other, these affected men now begin to operate by simply 'leaving' their true emotions "at home" - locked-up! Sounds familiar?

I know you've heard of women complaining that their men find it very difficult or are very reluctant to say the "I Love You" words. (I personally don't understand why this is an issue; a person should be allowed to say those words on their own - when and if they feel the need to, and never ever compelled to do so.) The preceding is most commonly the reason for such reluctance: they somehow believe that by doing so, it would somehow make them vulnerable once again. Therefore, as a subconsciously-driven protective measure, they avoid saying those words even though they may be feeling love at the particular time.

However, from this point onwards, these guys morph into what's commonly known to their friends and acquaintances as *Players;* and to women, after a few experiences where the guys displayed an obvious commitment to promiscuity, as "Doggs."

By age 25, most girls - now women - through experience and naturally developing more emotional stability as a result of maturity and hormonal-level balancing, start feeling the need to be involved in more steady, fulfilling, relationships - with visions of marriage, kids, and the whole settling-down thing. In western societies, age 25 usually marks the beginning of this *movement.* By age 30, women begin worrying about the ticking-away of their "Biological Clocks" as it is commonly referred to. What's ironic is, you would hear women make comments such as, "A good man is hard to find," "There are no good men left," and the most common of all, "Men are Doggs!" What they fail to realize is that the guys they *dumped* or discarded 8 to10 years ago - for whatever reason - are the same guys they are now trying to get to commit to a stable relationship and ultimately marriage. Good Luck!!

The situation outlined here may seem a bit outlandish to the average reader. You're probably thinking that if a girl or woman dated a guy sometime before, she would definitely recognize him and probably not want to date him again, right? I want to let you know that in practicing reality, it's not that simple!

Let's consider, for example, 10 girls and 30 guys living in a large City. Between ages 16 to 20, each of these girls dated 3 of the guys and consequently broke their hearts at different times. To give some credit to the girls, in light of their then emotional challenges in the way of what they thought they wanted or not wanted, as mentioned earlier, we cannot consider their actions as being deliberate in the strict sense of the word. However, if someone caused pain to another, whether deliberate or otherwise, pain was caused and emotions were damaged. What's important to note here is that it is not so much the pain that was caused; but rather, it's the emotional scars that were left as a result of the pain, the perceived heart-wrenching experience or experiences is what becomes the stumbling block.

To conclude: The 10 young women are now approximately 25 years old and now ready to be stable when it comes to men. It so happens that, coincidentally, each girl meets and consider dating, at different times, 3 of the 30 guys other girls dated and devastated as teenagers. Also, the 10 girls were never acquainted with each other, and neither were the guys. You can now conclude what the results would probably be. As the saying goes "What goes around comes around." And I would like to add, *whether we want it to or not!*

Let's make a timely disclaimer here, which, I might add, is probably in-keeping with your thoughts as you read through this chapter. I want to point out that the preceding situation is definitely not the experience of every guy on the planet. However, for the most part, the ones who endured the type experiences discussed here - or any other version of them - where deep emotional pain was caused at the hands of the opposite sex, are definitely the ones who usually lead the infamous "Dogg Pact."

# CHAPTER 2

## Who Ultimately Hurts Most When a Relationship Ends...Male or Female? Why?

Owing to the fact that there can be an endless array of reasons leading-up to and ultimately resulting in the untimely *break-up* of any given male-female relationship, the topic of this chapter may seem too broad for some to fathom the validity of any viewpoint that could possibly 'hold water' - except for an overly biased opinion. For this reason, I will limit my discussion here to one typical scenario, where either the man or the woman in a seemingly, internally and externally, mutually-loving, monogamous, relationship unexpectedly *breaks-up* with the other and immediately starts dating someone else.

The characteristic response of whomever the victim is in my above scenario, is the usual emotional hurt, bitterness, and the like – all of which we collectively refer to as being "Heartbroken." The question is, when this scenario holds true, which is the gender that ultimately hurts most - and why?

There's a common *saying* which goes: "Misery Loves Company." In my mind, this *saying* can indeed possess dual but valuable meanings. On the one hand, we can look at it as: in times of emotional distress, individuals who have experienced somewhat related issues in their lives – and have obviously survived them– are usually the best *sources of support* for the hurting individual. This sends a message of "You are not alone in this...." to that person; and so, most are able to quickly put the distressing situation in perspective, and *snap-back* – so to speak.

On the other hand, the above *saying* can be applied to people who we refer to as being "lost" or in utter known or unknown *misery* in some aspect of their lives, and somehow seem to invariably attract or cling-to other individuals in that very same - or related - predicament. However, here, the possibility of finding or discovering any solution(s) to jointly or singly overcome the so-called "Misery," is almost never viewed or even considered as being important in any way. So, paradoxically, depending on application, "Misery" loving "Company" can effectively help some to overcome the "Misery" they are experiencing - at the time - or, in-effect, keep some reveling in it to the point of seeing and accepting the prevailing situation as being *normal- to-life.*

*First, let's look at the typical woman in the* "Heartbroken" *situation.* Luckily, for most, *a Support System* is almost always in place to assist just about every woman who finds herself in *relationship grief.* What is this *Support System* anyway? This is commonly a group of like-gendered relatives or friends and acquaintances, who have been "in the same boat before," know of others who have been in it, or simply habitually acting on what I refer to as their *Engraved Woman's Kinship,* which, in our society, is commonly sparked, nurtured, and fully developed in *the circles* of girls, long-long before womanhood sets-in. The latter being the strongest source of support for women; but, at the same time, has also proven to be their most dominant source of misguidance.

What is this *Engraved Woman's Kinship* all about? As mentioned above, it is normally fully-functional "...long-long before womanhood sets-in" for most women. This means that all the sleepovers, weekends, girls-only pajama parties, and the like that we passively dismissed as *girls just being girls,* were the actual unidentified *Initiation Ceremonies,* followed by unrecognized regularly scheduled and unscheduled meetings for the bonds which is to develop into the seemingly sympathetically-biased viewpoints of women in support of other women in relationship dismay. They don't have to even know the particular woman....as long as there is an issue or conflict which has to do with "her man," she gets their support – no questions asked!

To the men: Have you ever wondered why every time you tell a story to your present wife or girlfriend, concerning any conflict(s) you've had with a past girlfriend or wife, how quickly she immediately takes the woman's side, long-long before you've even had a chance to complete your story? Also, have you ever wondered how is it at all possible for your present wife or girlfriend's verbal responses to sometimes identically mimic those of past girlfriends – especially the ones that occurred in the heat of arguments? I am referring to the type responses that made you wonder, "Do they know each other?" Or "Have they been talking behind my back?" This is indeed their *Engraved Woman's Kinship* – not only at work, but clearly on display.

However, although this "Kinship" and its related "Support System" is no doubt a good thing for women to have in-place in support of each other in *trying times*, to ease the pain and hurt of being heartbroken, and to further give assurance that life does go-on, outside of specifically *their problems concerning men*, this *bond* actually *does not* exist; it fails miserably! Why? Because, in practice, it is merely a put-in-perspective or maternal, conflict-resolving, "Support System" set-up to solely – as most men would conclude – "Bash men!" It's as if to say, "It's expected of them - anyway - so let's put this in place to help in the overcoming of it when it inevitably transpires."

The truth to this failure of *Kinship* and overall pseudo *Support System* - in other areas of their lives - becomes evident with the fact that women are continually competing against each other on all levels! Always! They compete on the grounds of fashion, success, *looks* – as in beauty; and especially so, for the attention of the very same men they collectively *Bash* when one of their 'kind' gets *Dumped* or hurt - in any way - at the hands of her *Man*. For example, typically, men believe their women "dress-up" in a provocatively sexy way *solely* to please them. Please! This may be partially true, on only very rare occasions, for up to a maximum of approximately 30% of the time. The other 70% of the time, this "dressing-up" is purely to provoke jealousy and envy in the eyes and hearts of other women. Believe this!

Also, unknown to some men, women discuss men among themselves much-much more than men could ever *dream of* discussing women. The disparity is mind-boggling! For women, this focus usually starts very early in life; and most times, by a very early age (lower to mid teens - usually), they have already developed and bought-into a misconstrued interpretation of boys (soon to be men), which is to grow and follow them throughout life. For instance, if you listen keenly to the undertone of most women, as they discuss men, you'd realize how much they keep *saying the same things* in so many different ways: "Men have no feelings!" "He has no clue!" "I don't even think he has the ability to listen and feel anything!" "He is like a Wall!" Etc. Instead of accepting men for who they are; and so, endeavor to *see themselves in the men* they supposedly love (Discussed in detail in Chapter 7), they typically resort to a life of incessantly *fighting against* what they're "conditioned" to want to change in men - not realizing that whatever we fight against *always grows*! In other words, the more we fight against something we want or desire to change in others, *the more things* we'll find necessary to "want to change" in them. It's an endless, unhealthy, uphill battle driven solely by Ego's demands.

In addition to the fact that women *do* discuss men much more than men *do* women - among themselves - women can get extremely graphic during these discussions. Whereas men would talk about their sexual encounters in a more general sense - leaving some things for *their* friends' *imagination to work with* (primarily as a consequence of *fear* and *insecurity* to some degree), women, on the other hand, would commonly break their men *down* into body-parts. And generally, discussions about their sexual encounters take-on more explicitly intricate *"frame by frame"* detail. In other words, they typically *leave NOTHING for their girlfriends' imagination to work with.* This common practice creates two potential problems with and among women.

First, even though there is almost always some level of embellishment in these stories, women don't seem to realize that the practice of *breaking their men down into body-parts,* and the further practice of sharing personal intricate details about sexual encounters with their men, only serve to pique interest and envy in the hearts and minds of their girlfriends. By this I mean, "interest" in their men, in the sense that since the details of what to expect would be seemingly clear ( and remember: *the grass always seems greener on the other side of the fence*), and "envy" or jealousy for what the particular girlfriend *may have* that some other girlfriend may think "should" be hers. Some have consciously and subconsciously bought-into the common saying that "All is fair in Love and War."

Often, many so-called girlfriends act on this type impulse in underhandedly competitive ways. Consequently, it has resulted in the destruction of many friendships - all over and concerning the very same men they are consistently trying to understand among themselves. Figure that one out!

Secondly, the habit of breaking men down into "body parts," has its own uniquely-added, subconsciously-imbedded, destructive element on women's viewpoint of men. Unknown to some, this habit of viewing men as "livestock" or "pieces of meat," only serves to create added disparity and confusion in their perceptions and appreciation of the true nature of men. What this does is it further solidifies the idea of men as being insensitive, cold, rigid, etc. Have you ever heard of *a piece of meat* that possesses feelings? Be careful what you ask for!

So, this is what women really have in place: A sort of *Support System,* which has been passed down thru many-many generations. And what I believe originally sparked the system into being, is the fact that women really *have no clue* when it comes to men; and never did! So, in light of . this, they have resorted to joining forces, as women, all in an attempt to work with and hopefully put into perspective or figure-out, this seemingly *confusing* gender. I guess they believe coming together and sharing their varied viewpoints and experiences, concerning men, would somehow lead to a clearer understanding of men's true nature. I have two words for those who think this way: Good Luck!

This need to understand and communicate with the opposite sex, is directly driven by the fact that we, as humans, have deeply instilled in our subconscious, an innate desire and need to commingle and share life with the opposite gender. I guess, simply put, it's just our nature at work facilitating procreation.

However, although this *Support System* women typically have in place is able to temporarily alleviate the pain and heartache they may go through at the onset of a deceitful break-up, most seem to be still left *lost* and very likely *doomed* to possibly experience *a repeat performance* of the same or related heartbreak in the near future. Among other things, this remains so, mainly because women typically come together and conjure-up their own personal, ego-driven, viewpoints of men's reasoning for doing what they do, rather than seeking-out and taking into consideration the viewpoints of men in order to include the male perspective in their final conclusions. This, I believe, is the missing link which, if explored, will allow women to gain a better understanding of the *full truth* when it comes to men.

It seems as if women think since they *blindly support each other* during these trying times, men would somehow do the same. However, they would be 'dead' wrong if that's what they're thinking. If a man is not personally involved, he would very likely have no reservation to share a totally unbiased male point-of-view, based on his own exposure and experiences. I know I would!

Therefore, as explained in the beginning paragraphs of this chapter, I think the paradox actually exists with most women. This seems to be the case, because even though for the particular situation they may receive some level of comfort and is able to sort of *move-on* from it, they rarely truly understand why they go through what they go through, so they keep on going through it - over and over again; and especially so, since no lessons are ever learned – usually!

Let me share a typical situation with you that I believe clearly exemplifies the truth to this. Typically, if a guy "breaks-up" with a woman - in her mind - "he's being himself; he's bad! Whatever!" However, if and when the typical woman "breaks-up" with a man – in her mind, once again – it's also *always* because of him: his fault, his actions, or his failure to act! It could not possibly be *her fault*; even though it may be completely centered on her actions.

To this end, I really *long for the day* when a woman would finally take some responsibility and admit, at least to herself, that the cause of at least one *"break-up"* in her entire dating life, thus far, was indeed her fault! I haven't had the opportunity to hear this admittance *even once* in my entire life of dating; *it's just never their fault!* I am not one to point fingers and label this response as one of deliberate denial, but, the truth is, most women *really don't believe it's ever their fault* in these matters. It's typically viewed as the fault of "The Wall;" the gender that possesses "no feelings;" the Man! He was not perceptive enough to understand what she was going-through; and so, didn't act sympathetically enough – in her viewpoint – in response to how she was feeling. This is the common judgment; although she may have failed to *clearly* communicate how she was feeling to him at the time. He is supposed to fix it! He's supposed to know this by gender! In her mind – as a man – *it is his job* to know!

Consequently, these are some of the defining reasons why women sometimes go through life *lost* in their *misinterpretations of men*, while, at the same time, continually finding it all so convenient to blame the very same *Men* for what they keep putting themselves through; and therefore, inevitably remain stuck in their "Misery."

The most peculiar thing about all this is the fact that it is women's extreme *misinterpretation of men* that serves as the *seed* which continually *germinates* into the "passing of the blame" for their *own* actions or lack of it, unto men. And as a result, history keeps repeating itself – generation after generation.

*Second, let's look at the typical man in the* "Heartbroken" *situation.* On the subject of men, it's quite a different story; but, stay with me, it does have an interesting twist.

Frankly, men really don't support each other in heartbroken situations. I cannot find better words to just put that out-there; they just don't feel or see the need to be support-figures for each other during such times. They just don't! Unlike women, who seem to support each other when in emotional distress, and totally compete against each other, otherwise, men almost always tease or mock each other when in emotional distress, and are always competing and sizing-up each other, especially where women are concerned, otherwise.

We can look at this seeming-reality with men, and ask the question: Why is this so? I think most of it can attributed to societal expectations, since men are *conditioned* by our system, which we commonly refer to as *our culture,* to be *macho,* to be strong, to be rigid, and not allowed to ever cry or show any feelings of being *hurt,* etc. As a consequence of this, men find themselves more inclined to tease rather than support each other in times of emotional distress and suffering. In fact, some men *cannot* and *will not* admit to their "boys" or any of their male counterparts, for that matter, if they happen to be in a vulnerable emotional state of mind, for example, because they *know* exactly where it would lead.

Again, one of the primary deterrents that keeps men them from sharing what they're going through with like-gender friends and loved ones, is this thing that keeps reiterating in their minds: "As a man, I cannot show weakness.....I *must* be strong - always!"

As a result, men fool themselves into believing they should always be *strong.* But really, what is *strength?* I personally don't think it's necessary to try so hard to be all that 'strong' as we call it. In my mind, it is indeed reasonable to show some vulnerability at times; and sometimes, what may seem to be *weakness* or vulnerability, may actually be *disguised strength* or vice versa - overshadowed only by our *Ego's concerns.* Nonetheless, let's look at this from another perspective.

In our society, if a man does not show his "strength" and tenacity, if a man is perceived as being "weak" and sensitive, he gets absolutely *no where* with women. The typical woman forever complains, though, how insensitive the typical man can be; yet, the fact remains, when he happens to be sensitive, she really doesn't want to have anything to do with him! This dilemma leaves the average man stuck in a situation where he cannot share his distress with his friends, since it almost always turns into a tease;

and really, who wants to be teased when going through emotional pain? And remember, being sensitive to her equates to not being wanted by her. So, as a consequence, men invariably go through their *pain* in solitude. However, this is not where it ends; it's usually just the beginning!

Clearly, it may seem as if he is alone, and it is the worst thing in the World for anyone to be going through by themselves. But let's examine what usually comes out of such dilemma. There is something called *self-reliance*; self- reliance in the way of *true strength*. You see, once you get entrenched in emotional distress and pain, and you're driven to the point where you can no longer look *without*, so you're inevitably forced to start looking *within* for answers, this shift will invariably take you to a place of what I refer to as, *radical independence, self-assurance*; in a word: *self-reliance*. And whether misguided or otherwise, the point is, you'll now start depending on *you*; you'll now start realizing that *you* are solely responsible for where *you* are, where *you* go, how *you* feel, and what *you* do and allow to transpire in *your* life - especially when it comes to women! In other words, you'll stop "passing the blame," and start taking personal responsibility for all of your relationship-based experiences.

This shift ultimately creates the type man the average woman, sadly, *does not want to have anything to do with!* She typically wants a man to be dependent on her; she wants a man to buy into her whims, to blindly support and give-into what she *wants* and *don't want* of him. The *very* last thing she usually *wants* is *an independent-thinking man*. Paradoxically, though, this is the type man every woman *should* want in her life. Unfortunately, her *ego's restraints* and childhood cultural conditioning, hardly ever allows it.

This is what has been created as a by-product of our system, or – should I say – as a result of the dichotomy of things in our society, where what seems as if it's going in one direction may actually be going the opposite way.

Further, in spite of all this, you'd probably conclude that men do hurt more. And on the surface, they do – in my opinion. They seem to hurt more on the onset of the emotional pain caused by an untimely *break-*

*up* or *heartbreak* – based on our scenario – when they are the victims of it. However, even-though some men may fall into the *cracks* and start embracing the heart-wrenching situation as the only outlook *life* has to offer and, as a result, are never really able to put it out, put it in perspective, and eventually gather strength from the *pain* they encountered, most are able to do so through internal reliance on self, instead of depending on a group-effort which *does* give some level of comfort and support - in the beginning - but usually never leads to any true lasting resolution.

We can even continue to say, "Ok, this is really what's going-on....but do we really want this?" Is this what we want in a society where men and women *must* interact with each other, and in a nutshell, *must exist* together and commingle in order to facilitate procreation, the necessary process to keep our world populated? Is this really what we want? I am sure it is absolutely *not* what we truly want; but unfortunately, it is what we have made into our *reality* – even though most of us don't see it. Most of us only see things at *face value*; but remember one thing: there is always an undertone; there is always an undercurrent going; and it's always either for *good,* or for *not so good.*

However, to re-state the title of this chapter: *Who Ultimately Hurts Most When a Relationship Ends...Male or Female? Why?* I hope I was able to open your eyes to some of the realities in life that most tend to miss. Further, I hope you were able to grasp, for yourself, where this contention really *holds water* – if at-all. I think my final analysis was pretty clear-cut; so here, I will leave it up to you to make your own decisions as to which gender you believe ultimately hurts most when these situations transpire.

# CHAPTER 3

# The Loving Nature of Women – Misguided

If I could receive a dollar for every time I've heard a woman say the words, "*I Deserve*" pertaining to *her Man*, and as it relates to what he's *doing* or *not doing* - in her opinion, I would be a millionaire today many, many times over. They deserve more respect! They deserve to be treated better! They deserve to be taken care of! They deserve a man who truly loves them - the way they "should" be loved! They deserve to be married! They deserve more romance! They deserve more foreplay! They deserve....! They deserve...! They deserve....! Why it is so many women think they are so *deserving* of what they're typically *not willing to give*? Is this really what they are: *Selfish from the core?* Or were they somehow programmed from childhood to act and feel this way?

We can, in many ways, equate this behavior to a helpless Baby that cries when it needs some sort of attention, because, for example, his diaper is wet or she's hungry or just plain tired of being in one place for too long. The Baby gets its needs fulfilled, and he or she is happy once again. Usually, the first time this comfort or attention is given, the Baby quickly learns that crying or other displays of irritability or discomfort, is the *sure* way to get whatever he or she wants or desires. In a short time, the baby expects this; and of course, nothing is required of the Baby in-return; after-all, he or she is just a helpless Baby.

It follows that this seeming insignificant infantile trait, which, incidentally, is a normal characteristic of babies, is sometimes actually mentally embraced and taken all the way into adulthood by too many of us. You know the type: it's the ones who seem to be completely convinced that the way to get whatever they want is to display discomfort and discontentment in the form of screams or complaints, or by showing signs of obvious irritability to a situation or circumstance that they expect someone else to change or rectify. Many women and some *shiftless men* fall into this category. They act as if everyone they know (especially those closest to them), somehow "owes them something;" but nonetheless, as with the helpless Baby, it is not necessary or required for them to give or do anything in return. This is a common example of how the "I Deserve" trait is given birth and *life* literally bred into it.

I used the term "*shiftless men*" above, only because of the way our society chooses to view this "I Deserve" trait when exhibited by men. A man displaying such characteristics will very likely attain only mediocrity in terms of success in his relationships; and the women who share his predicament, will totally avoid him for the obvious reasons. This will invariably become his experience; and simply because, traditionally, as our society sees it, "the man should give while the woman should always receive" period! This is unwritten law! As a result, most men who embraced this "I Deserve" trait into adulthood forcibly learn ways to subdue or dismiss it, in order to be remotely accepted as being normal.

It's amazing, though, how much our society completely accepts, effectively amplifies, and openly cultivates this very same trait in women. We even go as far as to encourage reinstallation of *the epidemic* into many who have long outgrown its self-destructive claws. Some of us even refer to it admirably, and with envy at times, as a woman being "Spoiled." The subliminal directive exists just about everywhere: at school, in Church, in the Media, at home, at work, at every form of social event and setting; and most debilitating of all, in the forefront of our minds.

Why is this trait considered to be an epidemic among women? I consider it to be an *epidemic*, mainly because of its contagious nature, and the fact that it has caused and continues to cause nothing but havoc in its path. What's even worse is that it inflicts what seems like irreversible harm on the ones who aimlessly practice it.

A very good friend, Jonathan, a short time ago, dated a young woman whom he was very excited about at first. (We worked together as Airline mechanics for a few years, and being born in the Caribbean, like myself, we became good friends and sometimes discussed our personal lives). I never got an opportunity to meet this woman; but to him, she was "The One" he has "been waiting for...." He told me that she was beautiful, sensitive, gorgeous, and owns her own successful business as a Financial Advisor. He further added that she views *life* and *love* in exactly the same ways he does and is extremely easy to talk to. In his words, "The first time we met, I felt as if I've known her all my life." Needless to say, I was very happy for him. I even caught myself feeling a bit envious at times.

After a few weeks, I one day saw Jonathan sulking in the hallway at work; there was a look on his face as if he just found out his entire family had died and was in utter despair because of it. I stopped immediately!

"Is everything ok - Man...........trouble in paradise?" I asked calmly.

"I guess you can say that!" He replied - in a somewhat dazed manner.

"I think I made a bad choice..." He continued, "But I'll survive...I did before."

After a little probing, Jonathan soon revealed that the woman he thought was so "perfect" for him, turned-out to be rather selfish - in his opinion. "Even though she makes about 3-times my salary" He added. "She expected me: *the man she thought to be a real man,* as she puts it, to pay for everything - every time we go out."

He continued to disclose that after he mentioned how much sharing the cost of their entertainment in the beginning clearly shows an unquestionable level of mutual commitment to their courtship, in addition to the time they were both investing in each other, she got extremely irate, referred to him as a "Cheap Bastard" and stormed-out of his apartment. Before exiting, he said she even went a bit further, venting such things as "As a woman ....*I Deserve* to be treated this way!" And "that's the way I was raised!" Needless to say, this ended their brief, short-lived, courtship.

Jonathan, like myself, is of the outlook that modern life involves sharing on all levels; especially so in a relationship setting. What I think bewildered him most, was the bleak outlook for any future with this woman. I believe he saw her mind-set as possibly manifesting into an outcome which could only lead to disaster for the then impending relationship; and rightfully so! Her actions were saying, "*I Deserve* to receive ... and not to *ever have to give to you......*and *you're responsible* for giving me the things *I deserve* - at any cost!"

Jonathan's love interest, which evidently "*went south*" for him, is not in any way unique. This woman, as many have done - and continue to do - will probably quickly move on. In short duration, such a woman usually finds a man who will be ecstatic to do and give *everything* Jonathan was not willing to do and give at the time. She would probably refer to Jonathan as above (when she cursed him-out) to every new guy. For some bizarre reason, women almost always find it necessary to share the negative perceptions they hold about other guys with new love-interest, as if to say, "If you want to get and keep me, these are the things you should never-ever do!"

Another phenomenon that remains rather common (discussed in Chapter 2), is the fact that women are almost *never* the cause of any past break-up in their relationships; it's always the particular guy's fault! Ever wondered why some women never seem to change their self-destructive ways? If the majority of men remain willing to accept whatever they continue to *dish-out*, what exactly would be their motive to make any changes? Think real hard about that!

Anyway, some men would pick-up on her demeanor as "fair warning," and correspondingly do the *extreme opposite* - just to gain favor with her. The woman, on the other hand, would not be realizing she has just given this new guy 'the ammunition' he needs to at least get past the *Jonathan's stage* of the game. Other men, those with some *self-integrity*, would simply view her attitude as a *red light,* and not pursue anything further with her. Still others would view her actions as entirely justifiable; and as a result, would very likely even add more derogatory terms to her *Jonathan's list.*

Well, this chapter is all about *The Loving Nature of Women......Misguided;*

therefore, here, I'll endeavor to explain the three typical distinct mindsets that drive the three different type men outlined above. Of course, this is solely for the benefit and awareness of the loving, but "*Misguided*" woman.

The type guy who plays the role of "*extreme opposites*," is classical! Surprisingly enough, he is usually very successful in gaining favor with the women. The only problem here is it's sometimes a total deception on his part. Rather than "be real," he would do whatever it takes to '*get-in,*' to secure favor. Frankly, I cannot entirely find fault with this approach; after all, who wants to take the path of *known resistance?*

In-effect, this type passively *plays* the woman against herself. Or so he thinks! As I alluded to earlier, when women meet unfamiliar men, who make them feel somewhat comfortable, they are customarily in the practice of telling their all. Don't ask me why? I believe they're somehow of the opinion that "a stranger," who they know absolutely *nothing* about and vice versa, is somewhat "safe" in some weird, uncanny, kind of way. Mostly, they'll talk and complain about all the things they *were* or *are* unhappy about in their past or presently-failing relationships. It's rather simple: The woman "*spills her guts*" about her discontentment with respect to her past or current lover, and *Bamm:* the '*new*' guy suddenly becomes the "perfect guy" in her eyes. Instantly, he'll start acting and behaving in a manner that reflects his interpretation of her true *wants* and *needs* based on her prior complaints.

Once again, it's absolutely amazing to me how such an approach or response seems to work so effectively on women! Is it because men are smarter, and women are 'dumber' or more gullible? Absolutely not! This happens, because women commonly allow their emotions and childhood belief patterns and codes to "*Misguide*" or cloud their judgment in a *HUGE WAY*! In other words, they '*play*' themselves; these men, simply recognize the path of least resistance and take it.

Most times, however, the situation may be much more complicated than this. To the average male, the above scenario is the exact process that seems to be unraveling before his eyes. Most women, on the other hand, may be seeing the situation in a totally different light. The typical woman would probably be thinking, "I *deserve* a man who does and gives me whatever I desire…. Therefore, this guy must be *God Sent*, since he doesn't even know me, that well, yet he's saying how much he wants to be exactly what I am *looking for* in a man…..wow! This must be *The One!*" She'd be thinking this - or some other version of it - totally ignoring the insight she provided just minutes, if not seconds, earlier! Ever wondered why so many women continue making the same foolish mistakes concerning their choices of men?

To dig a bit deeper…….As mentioned above, the average guy would be thinking he has just scored *BIG* with this woman. However, in reality, nothing would be further from the truth! Actually, he would have just played into her subliminal, mental, directive; the one she didn't even realize took effect. In other words, he would be thinking he's in *full control*, when, in reality, she would be *at the helm*, in full control of the situation. Unknown to him, he would be dancing to the beat of her *drum*. Where am I going with this? Let's examine the source of "her *drum*."

Subconsciously, just about every woman *wants* to be a *Princess*. This idea is commonly instilled very early in life when parents erroneously encourage their daughters to passively process such fairy tales as, *Cinderella* and *Snow White* to be life-goal objectives. It is at these susceptible times that the typical girl - soon to become a woman - starts believing that a *Tall, dark and handsome Prince, would one day ride into her life on a flawless White Horse and passionately sweep her off her feet with confessions of life-long love and affection. Then, in a state of eternal blissful love and grandeur, they both ride-off into the sunset….. And shall both live happily ever after.*

In addition to this all-too-common, inescapable, false reality or absolute illusion, parents sometime choose to further deepen the *element of truth* to all this by continually referring to their daughters as *Princesses*. This seemingly harmless gesture has been the pre-cursor behind many failed - otherwise blissful - men-women type relationships in our society. How is this so? As a direct result, these girls often begin holding mental images of *reality* with respect to one or more fairy tale. In other words, their self-image now begins to tell them that true happiness *ONLY* lies in them being able to "Live the Fairy Tale," as it's commonly called.

Sadly, these are the women who go through life relentlessly expecting to one-day meet a man who would provide them with the so-called "Perfect Life," as the fairy tales always depict. As soon as any man starts saying and doing the things which allegedly fits him into her mental image of what's expected of her pending *Prince*, she turns to *putty* in his hands; *Reality* takes a back seat, while *Fantasy* invariably takes over.

In certain western cultures, for example, it is customary for some young women to stay at home and do nothing with their lives in terms of pursuing self-sufficiency and independence, with the hope that this *expected Prince* will one day appear, and so bring life-long significance to their existence - in direct accordance with their innermost beliefs. Most never seem to ever come to grips with the fact that "The Fairy Tale" is *exactly* what it's supposed to be: *Wishful Thinking; never Reality!*

Nonetheless, many have lived their entire lives clinging to these images - all the way to the grave. After they meet every new, so-called, *possible Prince*, and the *bottom* falls out of the *Fairy Tale*, feelings of failure and discontentment take root. Then, they soon become the nagging, forever-complaining, disrespectful, girlfriend or wife. As they continue to embrace the resulting negative thoughts and feelings associated with their innermost beliefs, the "I must have it now - or else!" self-destructive inner dialogue with themselves - directed towards the man in their lives - expands to a point where something *must* give.

By this time, the affected woman typically doesn't really understand why she never feels sustained happiness in any relationship - even when all the seeming viable ingredients may indeed be present. She just knows this to be her reality! And strangely enough, the typical woman would find it necessary to blame everything and everyone - except herself - for her prevailing predicament. In her mind, everything about her remains 'on-point' or "perfect;" therefore, something must be wrong with *all the men in the entire World!*

Remember, in most *Fairy Tales,* the *Princess* is depicted as never-ever having to experience any situation in which the *Brave Prince* cannot vanquish in a second. In light of this, when any undesirable or unforeseen circumstance develops in any relationship that this type woman may find herself in, she would now - in light of her programmed beliefs - expect the particular man to possess *whatever it takes* to fix it. She may know, logically, that financially and physically, for example, it's beyond his means; but *fantasy* usually overpowers *reality;* and consequently, she will *lose all respect* for him as her *Prince* if he's unable to perform as she expects. In her mind, he failed to *step-up to the plate* and live-up to his "Princely Duties," which gave him *the right* - in the first place - to be deemed *her Prince.* This pattern goes on and on.

Just think: All this mental chaos, as a result of passively *misguided,* childhood-instilled, values. What a profound misuse of personal, God-given, power! Parents, please take note!

The second type guy would typically see the reactions of Jonathan's former love-interest as a *red light;* and so, will immediately become convinced that even the thought of dating this woman, would certainly be a total waste of his time and energy. Generally, this type represents the *not-so-typical guy,* who's uncommonly very comfortable "in his own skin." In simple terms, he's unwilling to temporarily - or otherwise - adopt any role or roles that are not in-keeping with whom he really is at the core of his being. It's the only way *Real Men* operate.

The *Real* or *true-to-himself* man, knows he can't change anyone; and especially so, a woman of such trifling demeanor. And why should he even attempt this up-hill battle – anyway, only to end-up immersed headfirst in her endless, forever-predictable, *Volcano of Drama* which every man despises? To him, it doesn't matter how "fine" she looks; in a few weeks, all of the initial enticement will become secondary, and it will be then time to deal with *Reality:* the real person behind it all, the real person behind the charade. Is it worth it? In his mind, the only logical answer to this question is, "Hell No!"

Just imagine, a woman just meeting a total stranger, and finds it necessary to refer to a past love-interest in a belittling way; and really, to prove what? "What would she be saying about me if we were to date each other and, for some reason, things didn't work-out?" To this type man, these are the signs of the type woman he won't be *caught dead* dating! Remember, we only have *one opportunity* to make a *first* impression. The above would very likely be this 2nd type guy's viewpoint. However, his point of view may not necessarily be driven by the harboring of contempt for the particular woman - in the strict sense - but rather, by the internal life-value conflict that her outlook on life created or induced within him. Suddenly, past encounters with this drama-based-personality-type are quickly recalled to the forefront of his consciousness, and the familiar expectation of nothing more but a down-pour of *drama-with-time* becomes apparent. Depending on his level of experience, most men with this type nature would not even bother pursuing this any further.

Nonetheless, in some cases, if the particular woman is physically appealing enough, the younger, less experienced, man endowed with this type nature may mistakenly think he can possibly "change her" for-the-better. Quickly, he would very likely soon learn that all his efforts were indeed only in vain! The truth is: some are so stuck in their ways, that even though they may be fully aware of the pain and havoc they have faced and caused, in the past, they possess no desire to change their ways of thinking and acting.

*Let me pause here for a brief moment to make one point resoundingly clear to all women. Let it be known: the one thing that turns-off and eventually turns-away any man worth having and keeping, is constant displays of any type of attitude that can be interpreted as DRAMA to him. This is not a joke! And as opposed to popular belief, it's definitely not an ego-driven thing! It's the one thing that would quickly drive the man you have - and want to keep - into the arms of another woman who makes it her business to understand his true nature. If you choose to disbelieve everything else in this book, make sure you take this to heart and believe it!*

Unlike my prior *"extreme opposites"* example above, these type guys are usually not very popular with the women. Incidentally, this can actually be *a good thing* - even though their Egos may prevent them from seeing the value in it. In this way, they'll be able to quickly screen-out "The Superficial," which may be more common than you can possibly imagine. Why are these men typically not very popular with the women? Let's find out....

Let's face it: most women *want to be lied to!* Some even – unknowingly – require it! If a man can predict what a women wants him to say and be, and *pretend his ass off,* he has her - express-packaged, and ready to do whatever he wants! I've heard women make such comments as,

"He could have even lied and say he missed me even if he didn't..."

A comment like this clearly shows that everything is about *their expectations.* It's not that they don't know it's a lie; the fact is they *want* a lie! Their predicament is, they want the truth, but they're expecting a lie. Therefore, if a man is not saying the things the particular woman expects to hear him say - whether it's about himself or about her, in whatever realm - his chances of being with her are reduced to zilch! This is precisely the reason why *Good Men* get passed-up every day; and why, women sometimes find themselves with men they really, really *don't want* to be with. Let's examine the term *Good Men.*

The term *Good Men,* seems to be used loosely by women and by some men (who choose to allow women and society to define their worth), to apply to those men who have endless finance and *completely willing to spend it all on a woman,* who, basically, *has nothing* to offer and is absolutely doing nothing with her life. Except for the temporary superficial beauty, which most men seem to believe at first to be permanent, some women conclusively *have no substance!* These men would marry them; provide them with huge homes and bottomless bank accounts; the *no-need-to-work* option; 3 to 4 vacations a year; and basically, *The Whole Nine.*

Some of you are probably asking yourself the question, "Ok! So what's wrong with a man doing this?" But before closing the book on this, let's look a little further......

In practice, the average male only realize what he has gotten-into after about 10 to 15 years or so have passed, and he's now *in w a y over his head*. The physical gratification, the money provided earlier, now becomes secondary, and *true reality* sets-in, the curtains are lifted. By this time, her physical beauty had somewhat *waned;* and incidentally - in most cases - his physical attributes, or lack of it thereof, was never really a factor as long as he had "deep pocket," and he is, as it is commonly termed, "A Good Provider" This is very, very real!

Suddenly, after all this and 2 to 3 kids later, they both begin to realize they had absolutely *nothing in common;* and never did!!! The fact is they never bothered to learn about each other in terms of their fundamental values. In other words, they never took the time to work on a relationship that could grow and *withstand the test of time.* Instead of being love-struck by him, she was being smitten by the money he has. He was overjoyed by the envious looks other men would give him when she was on his arms, and the fact that, for example, his parents said they "loved her" for him. She kept hearing from her family and friends how great a "Catch" he was. And, the list goes on and on. During all this, it never crossed their minds that what they were doing was *never, never, never truly for themselves;* but rather, only to satisfied the views, expectations and opinions of everyone else around them!

Initially, they were probably both feeling some sense of happiness, but for totally unrelated, unsustainable, reasons. So this most important discipline to life, *happiness,* never came to sustained reality for them. They never understood and appreciated each other from the core; therefore, as a result, the relationship failed - miserably! Remember, staying together does not mean the relationship hasn't failed or ended a long, long, time ago.

From my own experience, *the vast majority* would look at this and emphatically conclude, "Hey, that's just the way life goes sometimes!"

"There are no guarantees in life!" And "Some people fall out of love - you know!.......It's *normal!*" But before closing the curtains on this, we need to remember and further realize that no matter how we choose to look at it, *life is short;* we can never regain lost time. Situations like this occur much too often to be seen as *normal*, unless we're viewing *unhappiness* as a goal we should look forward to in our lives, and what's *common* should be considered as being *normal.*

As an example, consider the fact that the average American health starts showing signs of obvious deterioration at or about age 40. This is the approximate age when it's *common* to see men and women alike suddenly becoming afflicted with an endless array of life-changing, degenerative diseases, such as high blood pressure, heart disease, arthritis, acid-reflux disease, and many types of cancers - just to name a few. Also, whereas it was once *common* for cancer to affect individuals in a much older age bracket, today cancer is rampant among all ages. Erroneously, we are programmed to view these *common* occurrences, which primarily manifest themselves as a result of our self-destructive lifestyles - poor eating habits; lack of exercise; smoking; excessive use of over-the-counter drugs; not seeing the necessity to frequently cleanse our bodies - internally - of the numerous toxins we ingest everyday from our so-called FDA approved foods; using *Tradition* as an excuse to continue eating *"bad foods;"* etc. – as being *normal.* As far as I know, "normal" is, for example, when it rains outside *usually* gets wet. And if you deliberately or inadvertently put your hand in fire, you would *most certainly* be burnt. Etc.

This practice of seeing *common occurrences* as being *normal,* is largely due to force of habit, or as Dr. David Hawkins puts it in book, *Power Vs Force:* "Pattern Recognition." It's all about the way we choose to process life and our World. And here, once again, generational, childhood-instilled, belief-patterns come into play - forever directing our lives into self-inflicted pain, chaos, and dismay.

Let's now examine my interpretation of the assertion, "Good Men!" When I mentioned earlier that "This is how "Good Men" get passed-up…..!" I am referring to those men who are true-to-themselves; those men who have substance and integrity; and those men who respect and appreciate the women who complement these value-oriented traits about them. A man who fits into this category is honest about who he is and what he feels at all times. Here, I am considering "Good" and "Real" to be synonymous when it comes to men.

I've often told friends and acquaintances, alike, when they would become baffled and frustrated with the need or desire to fully understand some puzzling trait about their spouse or significant other:

*You should never allow yourself to possess any overwhelming need or desire to understand anyone else…..your purpose here - in this life - is to understand yourself, and to simply accept others for who they are!* I have actually blindly-given this advice, many times, before I clearly understood what it meant in its entirety. In my mind, it just felt like the correct way to be. However, this implies that we should make it our business to simply allow others to be who they are, as they are. If it's a love-interest or relationship situation, for example, and who they are conflicts with who we *want* or *expect* them to be, then it's a sign of impending compatibility disparity, frustration, stress, and the like. Should we opt to continue down this *death-ridden path,* we must accept that other person for who they are, or else, we'd be fighting a losing battle! Don't *ever* try to change anyone else; we can only change ourselves!

To paraphrase the words of Wallace D. Wattles, author of the World-renowned book, *The Science Of Getting Rich,* the term "Desire," in any realm, refers to "Directed mental energy or power - seeking expression." According to the author, this energy or power *should always* be directed inwardly to *oneself,* in order for *one* to achieve any desired goal. This aptly applies to every aspect of our goal-seeking lives; and therefore, suggests that we *should never* allow ourselves to become frustrated or stressed-out, for any reason whatsoever, by directing our energies to the *expected actions* and behaviors of anyone else.

I consider *frustration and stress* to be the extreme opposite of Wattles paraphrased definition of *"Desire"* above, which would now mean, "Misdirected mental energy or power - seeking expression." In my mind, this would be equivalent to aimlessly burning gallons of fuel on an open concrete surface. By doing so, all that we'll be gaining from the valuable resource is the by-product of wasted energy - *Heat!* This *heat* can be equated to the *frustration and self-damaging stress* we experience when we waste our energy and power by allowing ourselves to engage in such futility.

Put simply, if we understand who we are in terms of our desires: what we like or dislike; the things we want to achieve in life; and further grasp, that *only within ourselves* can we make these definitive choices to achieve and correspondingly bring them into full fruition in our lives, we would no longer feel the need to try and control anyone else. Actually, if our need to understand anyone else leads to any level of frustration, on our part, then what we're really feeling is not a "need to understand," but instead, a *fear-based*, ego-driven, "need to control" masked by the so-called "need to understand!" This *fear-based*, ego-driven, approach to life is a clear indication that we really don't fully understand ourselves; and therefore, we keep finding it necessary to blindly and aimlessly force others to fill this void we feel deep within.

As an example, there's nothing wrong with *giving* someone a compliment, or saying the words "I love you," if you're really feeling that way at the time towards another; however, *no one* should ever be forced to do either! It's simply not natural, and it takes-away from the spontaneity of the relationship and the moment. Coincidently, this is precisely the way "true-to-themselves" men view this issue. And largely, if he views life in this way, don't expect him to change for you! To him, if it feels *forced and unnatural*, he simply won't do it - whatever the consequence!

Often, women seem to be constantly looking for gratification in such things – *words*. If it's not said when and how it's expected to be said, then *The World literally just ended* - in their minds! For some puzzling reason, saying the words *right then*, and not a moment later, somehow makes them (the words) more real. The following is my take on the issue:

In my own life, I once dated a woman who after approximately two weeks following our initial contact, confronted me, in the middle of dinner, with the unusual question:

"So, what do you want from me?"

Shocked by the abrupt, *out-of-the-blue*, nature of the question, I paused for a few moments before replying......

"Why do you think I would want *something* from you?.........And, by-the-way, what is this all about?" I calmly asked.

"Ok! So I guess you don't know what you really want with me – do you?" She responded, in an overly accusatory manner, which was quickly approaching anger.

"Well, of course I know what I want!..............But at this point, we're in the process of learning about each other.....who knows for-sure where things will go? However, I do like the way things are going...so let's not force anything...." I concluded.

"Ok! Ok....Since you don't really know - for sure - what you want with me, I am going-to stay on my own!" She concluded.

So, basically, this woman opted to *end-it-all* before it ever really got started. Personally, I was a bit puzzled, at first, as to what could have possibly brought-on such unexpected course of action on her part. It was a little disappointing also, because of the fact that I was very much enjoying her spontaneity, wittiness, and overall *full-of-fun* type personality. Frankly, I am the type who believes in just *"kick-in-it"* (dating casually without definitive ties) when I initially meet a woman I admire; and therefore, allow things to take its natural course - without pressures. It's just my preference. The following is the reason why I prefer things that way.....

I've found that by taking the above approach, it allows us (the woman and I) to entirely be ourselves, by not feeling forced in any way to think about or having to meet any expectations of the other individual. If we *click* - it's all good. If we don't, we can definitely still be friends; no love lost. No pointing of fingers as to who said they *felt this* or *that;* or *who would be this* or *that* to the other; or *who promised* to be *whatever – whenever;* etc. None of that senseless stuff! If and when it gets to whatever it eventually gets to, at the time when it feels naturally *right and real*, then we can be and say all those things. I consider this approach the most natural and fulfilling way to be.

Clearly, the *misguided* woman, in my personal example above, seems to be of the type who is *forever seeking* for verbal gratification to promote inner feelings of being worthy or wanted, and to essentially provide her with *programmed* emotional satisfaction or comfort. Typically, this type does not really care too much if the words *said* are true or not; she just wants to hear you say them! More often than not, *Insecurity* is the driver behind such *urgent need*. Or more accurately, sometimes it could be an outward display of some deep, unresolved, inner emotional "baggage" from past relationships that probably failed on the *ego-driven* grounds of *empty words and broken promises*. The very same *empty words and broken promises* she now wants to hear more of. It seems as if it's necessary to coerce you (the man) to *say something now* that she can somehow *hold against you* later if it does not follow-through or pan-out. Talk about being a *sucker for punishment?*

Some women repeatedly have these experiences simply because of the signals they keep sending out to men. I thought my response to the question that was asked of me above: "So, what do you want from me?" was honest and full of integrity and positive possibilities. As is obvious, this woman conclusively picked-up-on or expected something quite different! Some men would have said what they thought she wanted to hear, just to prevent the possibility of conflict. However, that is not the way I operate! I will always be honest about how I feel - whether the particular woman likes it or not! At that point, I would've been insincere if I were to have said I wanted to spend the rest of my life with her, or that I was *head over heels* in love with her, or any of the like. I did see *viable possibilities*, but we were simply *not there* yet. I guess honesty is really not the best policy when it comes to some women.

As *REAL MEN*, we are looking at this phenomenon logically. Even though the woman above was clearly *misguided*, in her approach, she obviously didn't think anything was wrong with her untimely request.

It seemed as if she wanted to know - up-front - how far I was willing to go with her, primarily because of what she was feeling with respect to what she viewed as her *failure to clarify* in past relationships. However, my response was not what was expected or anticipated; therefore, she felt defiantly betrayed: How dare I betray her expectations?

In light of my above encounter and the ill feelings that usually result, I think it's a good idea for us to try and view every new relationship as if we're *learning to drive for the first time*, for example. With this in mind, individuals would no longer feel the need to rush things; and - like the process of learning to drive - will slowly allow themselves to understand and adjust to the personality of that other individual, which can be likened to slowly understanding and adjusting oneself to the controls and maneuverability of the particular vehicle, while learning to drive. This approach, I believe, will further prevent premature judgments of others, and will also very much increase the possibility of more successful courtships, and, ultimately, more successful relationships and marriages.

The third type guy outlined above: the ones who "…would very-likely even add more derogatory terms to her *Jonathan's list*," is sadly, the most common of the 3 types. In my opinion, more than 80% of all men in western societies fall into this category. This is the type that views themselves as *Powerless in the eyes of a woman*. For most, this *Powerlessness* applies to not only the particular woman they're involved with, but to every other woman they come in contact with - to some degree or another. Some would literally become physically weak and unable to verbally communicate in the presence of a woman they consider to be beautiful. And most believe, with deep unrelenting conviction, that giving a woman "what she *says* she wants" is the only way to "win her heart and love!" To them, when it comes to women, this is their *Bible!*

Once again, childhood-instilled, generational beliefs patterns remain the number one culprit at work here. Years ago when Dad said to you, "You must always respect women!…..Remember, your mother is a woman!" And Mom said, "If you want to make and keep a girl happy….you must always be nice to her.......be a gentleman!" Whereas words such as these were probably spoken *in good faith,* and are indeed good principles or disciplines to follow, to the juvenile mind - on the receiving end - words such as "...respect women," "...keep a girl happy....," and "...always be nice to her..," can take-on quite different meanings from what was intended. Remember also that, as a young child, the verbal directives from the adults in our lives can be like *"Gospel"* to us.

At such critical times in our development, our parents are typically the single most important figures of authority in our lives; therefore, just about every word said to us in an authoritative manner, from such source, would very likely be programmed into our subconscious as *absolute truths;* the so-called "truths," that may adversely affect our decisions and actions later-on in life. For example, words such as "...keep a girl happy....," and "...always be nice to her..," can be later translated to "If my wife or girlfriend is not happy - *for any reason.....it's always my fault......* since it is my duty to *always* keep her happy!" And no matter what the circumstance or whatever she does, "it's my duty - as a man - to overlook it, and be always cordial to her."

The above effect has also become *a two-edged sword* in our society, especially where girls are concerned. For example, if a young daughter happens to be in close proximity when the authoritative words are spoken to the young boy, she too would very likely be subconsciously programmed to *expect* the preceding from the men she'll encounter later-on in life.

In addition, notice that girls are almost always programmed "to expect" and "don't allow" - when it comes to boys. "A boy should always.......;" and "Don't allow any boy to........!" These directives are usually followed by a numerous array of what "to expect" and *"don't allow"* where boys, guys, or men are concerned.

Also, the above parental programming is further augmented by the *arsenal* of games and toys presently mass-produced, upgraded, and fast-approaching *reality* - with kids as the primary targets. As expected, the toys targeting girls generally represent some Prince-Princess type, Fairy-Tale-related programming. However, those targeting boys, on the other hand, usually possess a two-fold programming effect.

Firstly, the only tenderness programmed into the hearts of boys is toward girls. Now you know why married men are always saying, "My wife is the Boss!" These toys and games, though, never represent, show, or depict any semblance of controversy between the *Prince* and his *Fair Princess*. It's always the *Prince* against and vanquishing any pending or apparent danger to the *Princess*. In other words, *true reality* is always left out!

Secondly, the other boy-targeted games and toys are almost always based in *violence*: destroying stuff; crushing things with oversized trucks; war games; boxing; wrestling; high-contact sports; other forms of fighting; killings; and more killings; etc. The bulk of these games and toys are made for or by companies such as Disney, Microsoft, Nintendo, Sony, and the like. These companies - considered to be the so-called authority on kids *(programming that is)* - lead the toy and movie industry in this respect. As a direct result, these boys, which eventually become men, are programmed to solve all forms of adversity by resorting to violence! Have you ever wondered why men - even those in our government - tend to see and consider War and violence as the only viable solutions to adversity?

I consider the above programming to be the source fueling the following two broad negatives that typically plagues and drains the *life-blood* and *sustenance* from possible harmonious male-female, productive, fulfilling, life-long, relationships.

## 1st Negative: How it affects the approximate 80% males

I recently met with *a friend of a friend,* who sought me out because he had relationship issues that no one he knew seems to have workable solutions for. My friend, Andrew, referred him to me for some "tough-love, reality-based solutions," as Andrew likes to call it. Larry was born in Spain, but grew-up and presently lives in South Florida. The problem is Larry could not keep a girlfriend - no matter how hard he tried. When I queried about *his approach,* he informed me that he kept following all the rules his Mom taught him about girls. Rules such as, "to always be respectful," "to open doors for them, and to quickly give them whatever they say they wanted, so that I can always keep them happy!" But to Larry's dismay, the girls he dated always end-up cheating on him, verbally disrespecting him, or avoiding him altogether - unless, of course, the particular girl wanted or needed some immediate favor of him. In other words, Larry had no *Power!* He was in a sad, sad state!

Larry's problem was, however, rather typical. The only difference here is he opted to do something about the discomfort he was feeling as a result of the *contrast* he continually experienced with women. In other words, he continually felt displaced in relationships. I told Larry that the rules his mother instilled in him were indeed valuable guidelines to follow, but can only be effectively applied from a position of *Power.* With voice recorder in-hand, Larry immediately became very eager to learn what this *"Power"* could possibly be and do for him.

*"Power?"* he asked! "What do you mean by *Power?"* "What kind of *Power?"* He continued with an overly-puzzled, disbelieving, look in his eyes. I explained to him that the only way to effectively possess this *"Power"* - in the presence of a woman - is *to get inside her head.* How? By making it his business to learn what this *Power* is, and by constantly being this *Power* that *he is already* by default.

I further explained to Larry that this *"Power"* I was referencing, is not in any way ego-driven, because the ego is the source of our *weaknesses* rather than our *strengths.* The ego drives us to desperately attempt to make others see us as being superior, when deep inside we are really overwhelmed with feelings of being inferior. This *"Power,"* on the other hand, is borne in *Self;* and *Self* is that center of our being where our true *"Power"* lies. This *"Power"* is the outward emission or radiation of the level of *Unselfish Love* we feel for ourselves. This *"Power"* is evident in the way we carry ourselves. This *"Power"* is to know precisely when to stop being resilient without inducing fear. This *"Power"* is that level of centralized calm, self-confidence, self-assurance, and self-reliance that invariably attracts every woman we desire. This *"Power"* is based in poise. And poise is *Deliberate Self-Control* or *Conscious Power in Action*. This is the inner knowing that you unquestionably possess the necessary self-confidence and self-assurance you need, and to act accordingly. Using this *"Power"* is the only way to attract the true *essence of a woman*. Everything else is *pretense!* Money and fame, for example, may attract a woman, but the money and the fame will be the possessors of the *"Power"* - not you! Lose either, and there goes your *"Power"* - and your woman!

*As an aside: This issue will be discussed later, but let me make it clear here that women too possess and have access to this same "Power" (mentioned above) by default; that if properly applied, will attract desirable men to them in a way that will enable the cessation of the all-too-common DETECTIVE approach with men. Again, we'll dive into this issue later.*

When our conversation was over, I believe Larry did receive some useful advice, because he kept saying, "Wow! Wow! Thank You! Thank you! This is going to really change my life! Thank You!"

In a short time, Larry's life did rapidly change; he was soon attracting more women than he was able to keep up with. At the time of this writing, he was engaged to a fabulous woman, and continually gives me unwarranted credit for changing his life. In my mind, he's the one who made the necessary changes; I simply gave him some direction which he decided to follow.

I used Larry's story above primarily to make a point. There are far too many men out there who deem it okay to *push through life* with a mentally *"Powerless"* perception of *who they really are*; and especially so, where women are concerned. Remember, we cannot act in a way that is contrary to our deep-rooted beliefs; therefore, in order to change our actions, we *must* change what we choose to believe. That's right........what we believe is entirely our choice! Larry chose to make a positive change by seeking for some *tried and proven* advice. Luckily, he was able to get it and, as a result, his life changed for the better.

Again, some men really don't believe they have any *choice* in the matter; others do, but sometimes, still continue down the path that erroneously seems easy. "Easy" is commonly "The express road to destruction" – in my mind. The catch is, most times, we only realize our predicament after we're *already there!*

On my way home from work one early evening, I stopped at the local supermarket to pick-up a few things. As I approached the entrance, I couldn't help noticing an unusual couple in the produce section approximately 30 feet to my right. The woman got my attention at first. She was approximately 6 feet tall, well groomed, very shapely and elegantly dressed in what seemed to be business attire. In every sense, she was a woman who physically commanded attention! Every visible man in the store - including myself - gazed admirably in her direction.

About 3 to 4 feet following behind the woman - almost like her *shadow* - I observed a small balding man of not more than about 5 feet 4 inches in height, tagging-along with 2 *unruly kids* of between 2 to 4 years old. The man, oddly dressed in what seemed to represent business attire also, walked with an overly-slouching posture, giving obvious indication of his timid disposition. As he walked, it seemed to afford him great effort to cast his gaze from the floor to his forward path of motion. The woman pushed the shopping cart along as he followed with the kids.

In an instant, I observed the woman pointing her index finger in different directions as would a Drill Sergeant when giving commands to the rest of his platoon. The man responded by quickly rushing to every location she previously pointed to, and seemed to instinctively know the correct amounts of whatever the items were that she requested. I guess he had lots of previous practice.

Not once did I observe the woman gazing directly at the man, as she gave her commands. However, at the times when he looked at her I was reminded of the expressions I've seen all too often on the faces of kids in the many Disney World commercials on television when they see or meet Mickey Mouse. He looked at her with an expression of total *Awe!* It was almost as if he mentally fell to his knees in prayer and worship.

As the man continued trailing who seemed to be his wife, from isle to isle, constantly repeating the above activities, I soon realized the obvious truth of what was unraveling before my very eyes: *This man considers himself to be extremely fortunate to be with this woman, and she knows it!* Not once did I observe the woman picking-up a single item from any shelf! This chore seemed to be in-keeping with his subservient duties - along with the handling of the kids. His slouching posture was very likely the physical manifestation of his mental lack of self-esteem, and clearly showed evidence of the dismissal of his own personal *"Power."*

Sadly, this is the type guy who, I am sure, believes *deep* in his heart that *God literally smiled on him* by blessing him with this beautiful woman to *worship;* and therefore, this makes it acceptable for him to place the reasons for his life, his happiness, and his entire well-being or existence, into her hands.

In my mind, I deem it commendable for one to feel blessed to have a particular person in his or her life. But when this blessing is seen as a reason to *worship* that other person, it becomes grossly unhealthy. To see another person in this light, is to see oneself as *less* in every respect: less in value; *less* in worthiness; *less* in importance; *less* in everything else you can possibly think of! You are just as important and absolutely as valuable - never more, never less - as everyone else!

Feelings of being *less,* compared to another, further lead to other related feelings of unworthiness. For example, seeing your right to be happy and physically healthy as insignificant compared to that other person. Also, a common practice is for some to dismiss their own personal opinion as useless, in order to agree with that of another. What would be the need, when this other person *must always* be right in their eyes! In my mind, this is what *"worship"* means in the worldly, unhealthy, sense.

Furthermore, some of us fervently attempt to equate "Respect" with this "Worship" I mentioned above. They are absolutely not the same! Even though "Respect" for *Self* must also be included in "Worship," "Worship" is not necessarily included in "Respect" - in the strict sense. You see, "Respect" starts from within; therefore, you can't truly "Respect" anyone else unless you first thoroughly "Respect" yourself. And if you truly "Respect" yourself, you would never harbor the self-belittling feelings outlined above with "*Respect*" to anyone else, and especially so under the premise of "Worship!" Nor would you allow anyone else to be like this towards you; unless you honestly believe you are *selfishly deserving* of this so-called "Worship." This in itself is an outer admission of inner feelings of insecurity and weakness. *True Respect* - like *True Love* - is an overflowing of one's own feelings of respect and appreciation for oneself. When *Self-respect* - an integral ingredient in what we call *Love* - takes-on this direction, a harmonious, deeply-undeniable, mutually-gratifying bond between partners invariably results. When and where this exists, both parties are reciprocally uplifted without the lopsided effort described above.

You may be asking the question, "How exactly is his problem related to her?" Let me explain from the male perspective, and we'll get to the female viewpoint in the next section. His problem may seem as if it's not related to her; but nonetheless, it can affect her in an extremely deadly way! Understand that men, who view life from this perspective, typically see their women or wives as their sole *reason for living, breathing and existing.* Put simply, because the particular man's entire life-purpose becomes centered on this so-called *figure of perfection and completeness*, in his mind, he'll naturally begin harboring *unhealthy feelings of ownership* with respect to this woman.

These *feelings of ownership* are also commonly arrived at when women allow men to sustain their lives by financially providing them with their every need, while they keep-on thinking and believing that this is what they "Deserve as women." This route typically leads to these *feelings of ownership* in men much more quickly, for the obvious reasons. After all, she's completely dependent on him for everything; therefore, in his mind - and rightfully so - he owns her! This is the usually point where things can take a potentially deadly turn for women.

Without trying to whitewash the situation, it is very common for a man like this, who has been harboring these *unhealthy feelings of ownership*, to physically harm the woman he supposedly loves - her family, her friends, and even himself, if necessary - if he feels as if she might be planning on leaving him, is possibly *cheating* on him, or her family and friends are encouraging her to *'dump'* him. More often than not, driven away by his increasingly possessive attitude, it may be solely the decision of the particular woman to leave. However, being typically unable to fathom such possibility, he will find it absolutely necessary to blame everyone else in her circle. Furthermore, the possibility of infidelity more often than not may only exist in the mind of this warped individual, who has allowed *fear* to overtake his sanity. And remember, as outlined above, the way he was programmed from childhood: to handle all adversity *with violence!*

Here again, some of us may consider this to be uncanny or a little extreme; nonetheless, occurrences like these are very, very common in our society. For example, an ex-co-worker of mine recently lost his 2 sisters and his mother to a jealous husband of one of his sisters, who took his own life as well. We learn of these incidents just about every day on our local and international news. I guess we can refer to the ultimate driving force behind this as "Going Postal" in a relationship setting. The unhealthy emotional *bond-to-the-job,* which ultimately drives a person to "Go Postal" when faced with losing their "life-string of existence (his or her job)," is equivalent to the above *driver to insanity* in relationships: *unhealthy feelings of ownership.*

In addition, it is often quite common for men and some women to feel a *sense of ownership* toward their spouse or significant-other; especially so, when their love for that person is *based in fear.* And specifically, *fear of losing* that person to someone else. Most times, this *fear* comes from subconsciously blaming oneself for past relationships that failed for some reason or another; or from deep-rooted feelings of disappointment for some past unfaithful act committed against oneself. When the painful event occurred, the individual felt so extremely vulnerable, that the emotional hurt became vividly imprinted into their subconscious. It follows that whenever their emotions toward another approach the intensity it was at the time of the painful emotional experience, they somehow become *overwhelmed with fear* as the past memory comes to the surface as a viable possibility of repeating itself. In other words, this *fear* would typically be centered on the expectation and anticipation of re-living the heart-felt disappointment. As a result, this person may change so drastically to the other person - on the receiving end - that they may be driven to *make real* the very same *fearful situation* the other person is falsely reacting to. There is profound truth to the saying "Our Greatest Fear Comes True"

My advice is to dismiss these feelings as quickly as they come. It is normal and healthy to feel the desire to keep or stay-with the particular person we're involved with - if all is going well - for as long as humanly possible. Men are especially prone to developing possessive feelings for the women they supposedly *Love* and treasure. As mentioned elsewhere in this book, most men are naturally born with an instinctive need *to control their environment.* This instinctive need is often clouded or misapplied to take the form of *possession* when it concerns their women, and exists mainly as a result of ego-driven, childhood-instilled, belief patterns. As a man, it's a good idea to constantly keep these seeming naturally-occurring feelings in-check. They will come; but when they do, they are to be controlled and quickly diminished, or else they'll eventually control your actions; and the outcome is usually not very good. If the *Love* you feel for this woman is directly related to the *Love* you have and feel for yourself, then understand that these possessive feelings are not based in *Love*; but rather, in *Fear!* And you are above *Fear!*

However, it is very important for all of us (men and women alike) to understand that we cannot make or force anyone else to do anything they don't want to do! This especially includes staying in any relationship. If the other person wants to leave, let them go! We all know it hurts; but the reality is, *life does and always goes on.* Once again, if we allow ourselves to harbor feelings of ownership with respect to another, they can become extremely self-destructive. Also, let it be known and understood that *anyone* - no matter how sane you think you may be at present - can *indeed* become this deadly individual, if you choose to allow these *unhealthy feelings of ownership* to take root in your mind. Remember, any feeling of ownership towards anyone else is unhealthy!

## 2nd Negative: How the majority of women are affected

As mentioned and outlined several times throughout this book, the women in our society are programmed, in some ways or another, to expect *The Fairy Tale* from the men in their lives. The problem is, most are expecting this, but strongly believe it should never involve any effort whatsoever on their part. They *should* be kept happy by the men in their lives - by whatever means necessary! It is his civil duty to provide this! After all, it is clearly in-keeping with every *Fairy Tale* storyline; therefore, in every sense of the word, we can call this expectation "normal" for the women in our society. Some would even say with conviction, "Why not expect this?"

Presently, as it stands, this type mentality remains the #1 reason why so-called financially successful women are almost always seeking for men who are more financially successful than they are. To them, the opposite would be unheard of and completely ludicrous! Some would further say things such as, "Why should I step down?" In other words, it would be foolish for her to "step down," but she's always ready and willing to be "pulled-up!" Amazing!

Even women who are completely *void of all ambition* seem to think they *deserve* financially successful men; although - clearly - they typically have absolutely *nothing to bring to the table*. Despite this prevailing reality, to the typical woman, this is the one main attribute that will really give a man (whomever he may be) any permanent relevance in her life. This makes him "worth her while!" The mindset is, she is supposed to always be in a position "to receive;" and if and when she gives, it should be regarded as "A Treat," since it can never be erroneously viewed as "her duty" to give! In other words, it's "his duty" to give and "her right" to receive – and never, never, never, the opposite! This is, as a rule, the only *normal* that makes sense to her. This must be the underlying reason why the average woman who manages to achieve financial success, acts as if she expects *a medal of honor* for becoming so. *Please don't shoot the messenger!*

This deep-rooted, unwavering desire for *The Fairy Tale Life*, has also gravely affected the choices some women make for male life partners. My earlier supermarket encounter above clearly depicts one such example. The reality is, some would settle for marrying and spending the rest of their lives with men they are in no way, shape, or form remotely attracted to; but who are nonetheless, willing to "treat them" in a way that allows them to feel like the *Princesses* they believe that they are. Many, many, many, many, many women in our society have aimlessly made such choices - erroneously believing that *love and happiness* can somehow be *manufactured*! In fact, some entirely dismiss the possibility for true happiness, or for finding the *Love of their Life*, altogether, as a result of the 'bad' choices and undesirable outcomes of far too many past relationships that were, most times, driven to failure by the unwarranted pressures and excessive expectations they continually impose onto men. And so - with *frigid hearts* - they now resort to temporary *material gratification*, all in an attempt to somehow make-up for the *self-imposed suicide* they have committed against their own naturally-occurring womanly feelings toward men.

Further, as my supermarket experience above also shows, being married and getting every material thing she wants, while *throwing him a bone* every now and then (some sex) to keep him content, is the way things "should be" in-light of her failures. So, even though he may not be "all that," at least, she'll be living what seems like *The Fairy Tale Life* to the rest of the World. Very *sad!*

*She entered through the doorway, and immediately every paired eye - pupils dilated - rose to the occasion. How unusual! Her presence somehow seems to exponentially change the molecular structure of the oxygen in the room from $O2$ to $O4$ - and even to $O16$ - as it uncontrollably multiplies itself. Instantly, my food began tasting a whole lot better; and as if every other patron read my mind, a* *spontaneous pleasurable smile stretched across every face.......not excluding my own. Physically, she had average looks; however, there was something about her presence...something: An intangible force that somehow evoked visions of sharing life with this Heavenly Goddess - before my very eyes. Before a single word was spoken, these visions flashed through my mind at least 6 times....I counted! Every free-handed waiter and waitress willingly hurried to her aid. Despite all this - with a gratitude-filled smile - she humbly refused to take the best seat in the house for regular seating. That gesture alone immediately amplified my attraction towards her. And you may ask why? You see, it became clear to me that although she exudes confidence, self-assurance and complete inner poise; and evidently, constantly receives all the attention she could possibly want – the usual vanity and ego feeders – she was able to say, without words, "I appreciate all the attention of admiring eyes and virtuous smiles - even the 7 or 10 who attempted to wait on me all at the same time - but I never allow such things to get to my head, since every other person in here is just as valuable to me as I am to myself."*

This is truly a woman of *inner Power;* the type woman every man wants to share life with - whether he knows it or not!

On the subject of *Power*, it is a fact that women too possess and unquestionably have access to the very same *"Power"* discussed earlier. "Why is this *"Power"* so important" you may ask? Often, women don't use much of their own *Power;* and simply because, once again, they allow society, childhood programming, and especially *Tradition* to somehow dictate the way they believe they "should act" and be. As a result, women *seem to* give men too much *Power* to decide the direction of their lives.

Most would probably disagree with my conclusion here, since they often choose to maintain some level of control, but relinquish others, to the men in their lives, for what I call "selfish gratification!" This seems to be all part of *the plan* though. They only give-up some control at times when they believe they stand to benefit, but hold on to others, which unknowingly give them a false sense of *Power* or self-control. The extent of this facade is dictated entirely by the expectations of society and the unwritten laws of our government. If you're able to step back and see this exactly for what it is, you'll come to understand how it can and has ultimately and effectively destroyed the natural, God-given, *Power* hierarchy in relationships, and especially so, that in marriages.

Also, such women would further blame the men, if and when they fail to get the results they intended to get with the controls they choose to maintain. For example, it is common (traditional) for women in western societies to believe and act upon the fact that the man *should* be the one to initiate the subject of marriage. If he does not, then it must mean that he has no interest in marrying her (whomever she may be); and in her mind, "once again," she would have "wasted her time" with yet another man! This traditional view, or expectation to act, is *law* to these women. Therefore, to them, no other approach makes sense.

"Marriage is the prize to be secured; to hell with the relationship" as some would say. If the man is not initiating this conversation within a certain time-frame ( 2 years, passively set by society; or much sooner - if the particular woman is over 30 and approaching 40) - such a woman would aimlessly *walk-away* from a relationship with a man she claims to love deeply and up-until-then wanted to spend the rest of her life with. When asked, "Why the sudden urgency?" The answers I got almost always reflect the programmed response of, "I am not getting any younger!" Or "My biological clock is ticking away...I don't have much time!" Talk about having life all twisted! And the particular woman will further blame the man, once again, for causing the *Break-up* which she requested and vehemently enforced - all in an attempt to "force his hand!" Remember, *his sole purpose* is to make everything "right" for her; but only according to the way she sees it. And once again, "the way she sees it" is according to *The Fairy Tales* embedded deep within her psyche.

Can you see how this misguided approach clearly demonstrates a lack of *Power* in the women who choose to uphold such self-demeaning values? Let's dig further into the source of this - often ignored - *Power* possessed by women.

As an example of female *Power* and poise, let's look at a well-known figure in the movies and on TV today, *Angelina Jolie*. I believe it was mainly the effect of her personal *Power* that overwhelmingly attracted Brad Pitt to her. Also, I really never saw Jennifer Aniston as a woman who realized her own personal *Power*. Don't get me wrong, I think Jennifer is physically a beautiful woman - even more so than Angelina; however, Angelina has an undeniable, inner attractive beauty which manages to bring *The World to its knees*. Everyone I know seems to naturally love her. Have you ever noticed how she conducts herself during interviews? She seems to be able to always portray a constant calm, cool, collective demeanor. Also, there's an unmistakable *girlish, girl next door*, approachable type innocence and sincerity about her. In my mind, this is the epitome of the *Power* possessed by all women – if they learn how to become *one with it*.

I think the problem with Jennifer was that she subconsciously allowed our society to not only tell her what beautiful is, but also to make her feel all *so fortunate* to be married to the so-called "symbol of every woman's desire," Brad Pitt. Not to take anything away from Brad, but I can bet my life on it that prior to all this, Jennifer was probably harboring thoughts of Brad possibly leaving her for another woman, or that the marriage would never last. These thoughts, powerless as they may seem, usually manifest into reality.

It is fact that the radiated *Power* a person possesses is the main attractive force which sparks and keeps the interest of another. This is law! It is this underlying force which often leads to the phenomenon we call *Love*. The source of this attractive force or *Power* is based on *a deep and unselfish love for self*. Also understand that self-confidence and self assurance, for example, radiate an attractive force or *Power*, whereas fear and doubt radiate a repelling force or *Power*. Therefore, your *Power* can be positive or negative at any given time. A *dominant* positive *Power*, allows you to access and possibly keep the person you want in your life. With a *dominant* negative *Power*, you may be able to initially get the persons interest, but in a short time the *dominant* negative forces you emit will literally "drive them away!" What exactly is this *unselfish love for self* that results in this radiated, attractive, positive *Power?*

I consider *Love for self or Self-love* to be *The Unselfish Respect and Appreciation One Holds for One's Own Existence.* Unlike most people, constantly seeking for some sort of external *green light* from others to tell them when and how to love themselves, *Self-love* is *the only way* for us to sincerely feel, show, and express true or real love - not only for ourselves, but for all others as well. It is the only true source of our self-confidence, self-assurance, self-reliance, poise, and all other self-forces; unfailingly leading to success and abundance in every walk of life.

This *Power*, as mentioned earlier, is from *within* only. Again: This *Power* is only from *within.* Therefore, we cannot exert demanding verbal force of any kind unto others, and expect them to act in a way that will *make* us feel *Love* for ourselves. If that's what you're doing, then it is the reason why your relationships never-ever last; you've been experiencing a *fictitious sense of Love.* All your possibilities for true love and happiness exist only within you! That's where it begins and ends! Nothing outside of you can make you feel *sustained happiness* – or *Love!* After you fill yourself-up with this *Self-love*, it is only then that it can *unselfishly* overflow unto others. Outside of this, you will find yourself making uncanny demands of others under the pretense of a false sense of Love or *Attachment.* Therefore, you cannot truly Love anyone until this *overflowing* occurs! "My cup runneth over," as the Bible says, specifically applies here.

Some would say, "I'll feel like this when I get *this thing* or *that thing* in my life!" Ok! Does this mean you're willing to *hold-off* on loving yourself? Please let it *sink-in:* you cannot really feel love for anyone or anything unless you truly and deeply feel love for (respect and appreciate) yourself; and loving yourself, is not arbitrary. In other words, it's not one thing for you, but something else for another. *Love*, like *Truth*, is *NOT perception* - as some of us like to regurgitate. True self-love or *Power*, lies in us adhering to the principles and disciplines set-forth by our *Creator.* The more aligned we are with these principles and disciplines, the greater our potential for a happy and fulfilling life. "He that is within you is greater than he that is within the World!" When we start living from this vantage-point, everything in our World and everyone in it will start fitting and falling into place like a picture puzzle we've been working on all our life.

To the *Loving,* but *Misguided* woman, I want to add a word of advice here. Just as it is natural for women to often feel *chilly,* most of the time, and sometimes need a sweater or a blanket to keep themselves warm, it is also natural for women to need some level of guidance from the men in their lives and vice versa. And of course, men in-turn do need guidance from God or Supreme or Universal Intelligence – which ever term you choose to use. I do believe within myself that this is the natural hierarchy set-forth by God to allow us to maintain proper balance in our personal relationships.

This does not mean that women don't need direct guidance from God also. All it means is that in order for a man to be *The Man* that God intended him to be, he must effectively assume his rightful role. The God-given nature of every woman requires this. Every woman who has realized her rightful *Power* will tell you, without reservation, how much she relies on her man for a certain level of guidance that only a *True Man* can provide. This guidance is embedded in his presence, his demeanor. Unlike the false material security that most women seek to replace it, this guidance is the true safe-haven which allows for a woman to feel truly secure and fulfilled in any man-woman, monogamous, relationship.

Let me make a timely disclaimer here: *This guidance has nothing to do with control!* It is a *passive influence* that only *The Logical Gender* possesses. That's how God intends him to be for - and to - his woman. In western societies today, this intrinsic trait has been for the most part, subdued, muffled, and mostly obliterated in men - only to the unrealized detriment of life-long, otherwise healthy, relationships. It is only after this naturally-occurring male trait is openly embraced and nurtured by women that men would become equipped with what it takes to accurately recognize, appreciate, and cherish the sensitive emotional beings that they are. In other words, a man cannot be sensitive to his woman's naturally-occurring self, if his naturally-occurring self is constantly being down-casted and subdued by her! When this is in place, he would be empowered by her and she in-turn empowered by him. The outcome can be phenomenally gratifying on both sides.

# CHAPTER 4

# The Loving Nature of Men - Misinterpreted

Men are among the most misunderstood of all beings! Unfortunately, this is especially so by the ones they hold closest to their hearts - their women. Although bold, this statement is in many ways indisputably factual. To this end, I believe it merits profound consideration here, since - in my mind - it remains the number one overlooked reason behind the continual destruction of the family nucleus in western societies.

What seems to be perpetuating this deep-rooted misunderstanding is the fact that women tend to believe that they undoubtedly *know* men and have thoroughly figured them out. Often, the mistake they make is they are incessantly trying to *figure-out* men through their own *misunderstandings* of themselves; and generally, conclude that the things men do and the way men act, react, and interact are all due to the very same reasons that they would do the same – whatever it may be. However, nothing is further from the truth!    When I was very young, I found myself in a mind-boggling predicament. Everything about girls seemed extremely puzzling to me: Their viewpoint on life; their likes and dislikes - as I perceive them to be; the kinds of guys they'll go *head over heels* about; and the most puzzling of all, I couldn't understand why '*the hell*' I found myself so intrigued, fascinated, and overly attracted to them! To sum it all up: girls just didn't make sense to me! Faced with this dilemma, I made it my intention to learn as much as I possibly could about girls. In other words, I became obsessed with attempting to understand what really made women *tick?*

At first, the challenge seemed hopeless! Initially, I concluded that in order to understand girls, I must first understand myself. Although useful in many ways (as I found out later), I believe I was trying to apply the principle too early in life, because this approach took me even further *into the red.*

Later-on, it began to become more and more obvious to me that guys and girls were naturally and fundamentally different in many ways. The reality of this truth - except for the obvious physical differences – soon became a real *eye-opener* for me.

Then one day, out of what seems like nowhere, the truth suddenly came to me: *I should first try to understand the reasons why girls think the way they do, and the clear knowledge of this reasoning would be the first necessary step towards gaining a clearer understanding as to why they act, react and interact so much differently than boys do.* This approach was completely life-changing for me.

I know you've probably heard women complain about how much they've given their men *everything* they could possibly want to "make them happy," and they still cheat or have cheated on them – right? Strangely enough, if you were to *pull* these men aside - one-by-one - and somehow inquired into whether they've ever had any such discussions between themselves and their women or wives as to what would or would not "make or keep them happy," their answers would very likely be a resounding *"No"* for the majority. If a woman really wants to know and understand what makes and keeps her Man "happy," she should simply ask him! And this next step is very-very important: when he answers, she should try to listen, instead of contaminating his response with what she *thinks* he *should* have said – or meant.

Men are mostly logical beings; therefore, "Real Men" usually want nothing more than to let their women know exactly what it is that *makes* or *keeps* them happy. In their minds, this somehow gives lifelong relevance to that particular woman.

I am sure, after reading the last few paragraphs, some women may probably react with some version of, "I don't need to know what makes him happy.... I am the one who needs to be kept happy!" Believe it or not, there are women who actually *think* in these terms *only*; and simply because they believe it's the correct way to *be* by default of being a woman – according to the prevailing, subconsciously-instilled onslaught of behavioral directives many have adapted. Even though some may disagree, this way of thinking is indeed *always* learned.

Even so, most men I know - including those I've interviewed at lengths - claim that they constantly strive to understand what *makes* and *keeps* their women happy. Almost invariably, the men proclaim that what *makes* their women happy seems to incessantly change from minute to minute and from day to day.

Consequently, a "Real Man" relies on his woman's actions and reactions *to him*, to decide on what he believes she really *needs* and *wants*, instead of listening-to and acting-upon what she "says" she *needs* and *wants*. He is able to do this, simply because he understands her true nature. Even though the typical woman may protest, at times, she would not readily leave a man who has tuned-into her *true self*. Unknown to some, a woman *needs this* in a man in order to feel secure and complete in any relationship. Why do you think the so-called "Bad Boy" image gets so much respect and notoriety all at the same time?

As an aside: I've used, and will be using, the term "Real Men/Man" several times; therefore, I think an explanation is in order here. It is fact that some men don't seem to identify with their God-given power and *right* to be in control of their environment. *Being* "in control of their environment" *refers to being in control of one's own actions and reactions to things and circumstances, from a self-directed, logical, inborn, perspective - rather than always responding and adhering to what's passed along as supposed truths, or proper codes of conduct.* As a result, these men typically go through life under the pretense of a false reality. As a direct by-product of cultural codes and other misleading childhood influences, some men actually live-out their entire lives adhering to the belief system which dictates that all a man needs to be to his family is a "Good Provider," to the extent that he should provide money like a bank - with endless availability of funds.

He must do this, by whatever means necessary, in order to be tagged or viewed as a "Real Man" in their eyes.

This cliché has long outlived its relevance in modern times. In our ever-growing economically and financially challenging World, it has become absolutely necessary to have dual incomes in most married households. In light of constant corporate down-sizing and building stress levels in the workforce as a result of single employees now carrying-out the duties and responsibilities today equivalent to as much as five employees only a few years ago, it has become the only sensible thing for families to do.

In spite of this, some women are reared to believe that a *self-respecting goal for a woman is to not work!* Why? The ultimate goal for some, is to find a so-called "Good Man," which, incidentally, also means - as outlined above - a man with lots of money so that the particular woman in question can stay at home, shop, travel, watch television, shop some more; and maybe someday, learn how to cook and possibly bear him some kids - if she thinks he *deserves it.* With this mentality fully acceptable and thoroughly accepted on both sides, the typical man can never be the true leader in his relationships, and wonders why he's constantly faced with failure after failure in his efforts.

Also, the society we live in passively dictates that a man's responsibility (and especially so a married man's) is to *worship and praise* his woman or wife (*The Fairy Tale directive*), but should never, in any way, shape, or form expect or demand the same in return from her. It's just what he must do to be considered a "Good Man!" Culturally, this unwarranted, traditional, self-inflicted *sword* has been accepted, digested, assimilated, and perpetuated for countless generations - with no signs of ending any time soon. Sadly, the vast majority of men accepts this dogma as *truth-to-life*, and correspondingly clings to it as would a drowning man to *the silhouette* of a straw.

To continue: Women, on the other hand, typically want their men to *always* be agreeable with respect to what they're *expecting* their answers *to be* to questions or opinions, for example, when asked of them. Unwittingly, these expected answers or opinions usually pertain to the particular woman's viewpoint only. By default, the woman typically takes for granted that her man *should* somehow *know* her well-enough to answer in a manner that is in-keeping with what she *expects* - even though it may not be in-keeping with his true viewpoint or opinion on the particular issue. In other words, his personal viewpoint often seems irrelevant to her. She assumes *Her Truth* to be fact, and acts upon it as such.

As an example, the great majority of women seems to think that all a man wants to *keep* him truly *happy*, is some regular sex; while, of course, they *run the show* and get all their list of needs and desires fulfilled. The typically woman, however, becomes puzzled, disappointed, and even hurt when she finds out or realizes that her assumptions were completely wrong! Her usual initial mental reaction is to blame the particular man for being deceitful - even-though she may have been busy deceiving herself with this *false truth* all along. Once again, this act of almost always seeing themselves as being *blameless* in these circumstances is - in my mind – is one of the primary, underlying causes of dysfunctional relationships and marriages.

Consider, for example, a couple having a disagreement over dinner or a heated difference in opinion about an episode of a TV show. For some, if she didn't emerge victorious or 'win' the argument – as it is usually viewed by them – then she would become *off-limits* to him, sexually, that particular night. This may even last a few days, depending on how much *punishment* she chooses to inflict on him for not allowing her to 'win.' In her mind, if she keeps him from being "happy," he would *know next time* to allow her to 'win' - *at all cost!*

This practice has been - and continues to be - somewhat of an *epidemic* in our society. It's commonly known as "Putting him in the Dog House." Even though most men speak of it jokingly among friends, being in the "Dog House" is no fun, and can actually destroy the very fabric of the particular relationship or marriage. How can anyone outwardly expect another to be agreeable to their opinion, even-though he or she knows it's not the way the other person really feels? This has got to be the most selfish, egotistical, gesture known to man! What some women don't grasp is that maybe the reason why it seems as if sex is the only thing that keeps their men *happy*, it's simply because *nothing else* about them really does!

Often, faced with this common dilemma, the majority of men learn quickly not to be confrontational in potential argument situations; mainly to keep the peace, and to get their regular *sex fix* – as most have allowed themselves to be identified with. Remember, a man logically develops and feels love for a woman based on how she reacts towards him. So, in an unselfish way, he may be *blaming* himself for her actions. The mistake here is the typical man allows himself to be stifled. This stifling of a person's viewpoint or opinion in any relationship, if left unchecked, leads to unrecognized stress, discontentment, and ultimately, utter resentment towards that person ( the one actively engaging in the stifling) on a subconscious level. Ever wondered why married men usually *die-off* at a much younger age than their wives? I think we may be on to something.

So, as it stands, some men - married or otherwise - are misled into believing they *Love* and *crave* sex much more than their female counterparts. What they fail to grasp is that their women actually *Love* and *crave* sex just as much - if not more; but the catch is, they *love* and *crave Control and Power* much more than they do sex! Typically, they'll sometimes sacrifice the joy of sex for the perceived power of keeping their *Man* on a short leash, like a hungry dog with food served but leash not long enough for him to enjoy it.

What gets me, and what the great majority of men don't seem to get, is that the more they allow themselves to be controlled by the *sex-act* between themselves and their partner, the less of a *Man* they can be. And very soon, their *God-given-right* as Head of The Household (Leader of The Relationship) will be circumcised to *nothing* - in all areas of their personal lives. Further, *it is fact* that when such a point is reached, the same woman, the one who is constantly pushing the particular Man in this self-diminishing direction, can't help herself but to *lose all respect for him* as a Man.

This resulting, seemingly-contrived, reaction would not in any way be a deliberate course of action on the part of the woman; it's an integral part of her fundamental make-up to become thoroughly disgusted with any Man at such a pivotal point in the relationship. Basically, she'll be left with *nothing to fight for:* no mystery, no intrigue - when it comes to this particular man; and as it follows, she'll further lose all *attraction* and *desire* for him in every possible way! Believe this!

Therefore, what this is revealing to us is that the man's unselfish, loving act of giving-in "to keep the peace" and allegedly keep his woman "happy," ends–up turning her away from him and usually into the arms of another Man - with a *backbone!* Sounds scary? In practice, this actually happens more often than you can possibly imagine.

Personally, I consider the above to be one of the leading underlying reasons for infidelity in women; both in marriages and otherwise. In some cases, the process may not always be initiated by the above circumstances; nevertheless, when any man *loses* his manhood, by giving-in to *everything* and standing-up for *nothing* in a relationship setting, he's, in essence, destroying the respect and desire which that woman holds for him, and consequently, the longevity of the particular relationship. Put simply, every woman desires and deeply needs a "Strong Man" in her life! She may verbally request otherwise, but only a "Real Man" knows the truth to this.

Conversely, some men in long-term relationships - including marriage - sometimes don't even understand why they *Cheat* or possess a burning desire to do so - if the opportunity permits. For some, I believe it may be their underlying pent-up feelings of discontentment and resentment that is partially, if not wholly, responsible for them eventually taking this course of action.

Even though most of the men interviewed during my research didn't say it out loud, their general demeanor was somewhat of a lashing-out against a situation (or situations) which continues to make them feel *Powerless.* Invariably, this seems to be the one main reason why men – especially married men – *Cheat,* and find it all so necessary to spend excessive amounts of time and money at *Strip Clubs* - or the more refined, politically-correct, name *Gentlemen's Clubs*. Often, in one breath, they'll be speaking of their wives rather favorably; yet, in another, they'll be speaking of them almost as if they were residing with live-in enemies. Strangely enough, the men who displayed having more "Personal Power" in their relationships spoke of their wives more favorably in all respects.

I think women need to recognize that men are leaders by nature; and so, are born with an inherent need to be in control of their environment. A man - by virtue of his nature - seeks success in everything he desires. For example, he cannot feel *in-control* or *successful* in his endeavors, if he's constantly being stifled or downtrodden by the one whom he most seeks refuge, gratification, acceptance, and love. It is, without doubt, a *cut-throat* World we're living in; therefore, the typical man views his home and family as his *Haven*: A place of peace and tranquility; a place where he's allowed the serenity to regroup. This is what I believe he craves most so he can be strong and ready, in both mind and body, for the next workday. It's not just a desire; it's a need! It's the main role his woman or wife *needs to play* to keep all of his focus *at Home;* or more accurately, on their relationship. It is the only way he is able to be the very best *Man* that he can be in and for the relationship.

Isn't it sad that some men seem to think all that ever come out of their wives or women mouths is a constant.. "What about me? What about me? What about me? What about me?" Whether a woman agrees or disagrees with what the man seems to be interpreting from her actions, is beside the point! If he's somehow getting the wrong signals, then she should make it her business to clearly and honestly explain her motives to him. This goes for men too. Both men and women must come to realize that proper communication in every relationship is directly related to the accurate interpretation of the other partner's actions, words, etc. This is only possible, when partners are willing to "break it down" for each other. We can't expect others to read our minds. Women, especially, seem to uphold a very high value on this ridiculous notion. It simply does not work!

Often, when emotionally charged or discontented about a particular situation, some women would say one thing but yet mean quite another. In my own life, for example, I once dated a woman who abruptly voiced to me on the phone one day that the relationship was not *working-out* for her…so she wanted *out*! I quickly acknowledged her request, and promptly ended the call. At that time, I was working on a very important business project, which significantly limited the time we were able to spend together. Of course, I was rather disappointed about her request; but in my mind, this was obviously something she thought about, at lengths, before making the decision to share her final conclusions with me.

Approximately 5 minutes after I ended the call, my phone rang once again. I answered,

"Hello!"

"Is this the way you want this relationship to end?" She accused….in a loud, trembling voice.

"I can't believe I wasted four months of my life with you!" She continued…in a blameful, offensive, manner…..now in obvious tears. "I said what I said and you just accepted it without asking me why…I now understand……. you really don't care!" She concluded.

To the misguided woman: In short, to keep a man truly happy he needs to feel wanted and respected at all times. Remember, *respect* does not only mean you choose to not use *profanity*. By the same token, being "wanted" does not always or only refer to *sexual desire*.

On the flip side, due to cultural codes and other childhood instilled mental programming, some misguided men tend to misuse or erroneously apply and utilize this "need to control their environment" I referred to earlier. When I use terms such as "…Head of The Household" and "…controlled by the sex-act…" and "…..in control of their environment," I am not implying that men should be *Tyrants,* or be disrespectful, or what we refer to as "rude" in anyway to their female counterparts. A *Real Man* respects himself first; and if he does, it becomes natural for him to respect everyone else – especially so, the one whom he loves. Showing respect is not a sign of *weakness;* however, the lack of *respect* definitely is!

Consequently, this may very well be a major part of the disparaging Love problem in our World Society. Some of us view our *Love* for someone else as a "right to control" that person; and further, *fool* ourselves into believing that we're somehow "protecting our own interest" by *making sure* we're not "deceived" by that person, or allow anyone else to "take them away." Let it be known: this entire thought pattern is rooted in nothing else but unadulterated FEAR! FEAR, if left unchecked, can *only* become destructive - both inwardly, to oneself, and outwardly, to the ones we supposedly claim to Love and cherish. We must make it our business to look FEAR 'square' in the eye and DISMISS IT!

In order to dismiss or dissipate FEAR, we *must* calmly accept the things we FEAR most as *viable possibilities*. In other words, we must see what we FEAR most as possible; but nonetheless, powerless in disrupting our existing well-being. A powerful, FEAR-dissipating, affirmation can be something like the following: "I may not be able to control *the outcomes*, but I can definitely control *my reactions* to them! I know that FEAR is only an illusion; therefore, I have absolutely nothing to FEAR - EVER!" This conscious act alone will afford us the immediate personal power we need, and, at the same time, provide us with the inner ability to remove whatever we FEAR most from the forefront of our thinking. It is only after we're able to take this stand, would we gain what it takes to transcend the crippling grip of FEAR, and so, further able to move towards experiencing and achieving a truly harmonious state of trust and well-being in our relationships. Indeed, if we continually focus on what we FEAR most, we're actually *willing-it*, or *them*, to become our reality. In my mind, being in any state of FEAR - in any respect - is certainly the single most self-destructive, weakened, state of being there is!

Remember, trust and love starts from within. It's only after we learn to trust and love ourselves, can we then obtain the discernment to *truly* trust and love anyone else. This does not guarantee that others won't deceive us; it simply means that the trust and love one holds for oneself, will afford them the ability to put deceit and disappointment in proper perspective, and quickly move-on – if and when they occur. A good concept to keep in mind is, we cannot "make" anyone do, want, or feel what they don't want to do, want, or feel. Please let this sink-in!

As a man, one should see oneself as somewhat of a Lion: confident, well rounded, strong, and powerful; yet tender and truly loving – in all respects. True *POWER* is not a conscious, constant, display of strength and will-power; true *POWER* is a *PRESENCE; an AWARENESS*. This presence, commands and induces, respect, honor, admiration, and powerful feelings of desire in the opposite sex, for example. It comes from first identifying with one's own true nature as a man; and from further realizing, that a well-rounded man harbors absolutely no FEAR within himself! Remember: you're in control of your environment; FEAR says you've *LOST* this control!

Often, men seem to be more outwardly-expressive about their inner feelings of desire than women are. This is especially so in the physical sense. It is the one main reason why men continue to be misjudged and, to some extent, controlled by women. During the early stages of courtship, for example, men are frequently more explicit about their physical feelings of desire - either by the use of words, or by tell-tale body-language - often readily picked-up by the average woman. As a result, women sometimes end-up *shooting themselves in the foot* by prematurely destroying the possibility of many great, life-long, soul-mate-type relationships. They would make comments such as, "I caught him looking at my ass....so he must only be interested in having sex with me..." Or "He told me I was very sexy on our first date......why is he thinking about sex so soon...?" Or she just met him and never bothered to discuss how late he's allowed to call, and he inadvertently called after 10:00 pm once, which she blamefully viewed as him setting the stage for upcoming "Booty Calls (calls to come over late at night for the purpose of having sex only)."These are the foolish things some women would discuss with girlfriends just prior-to or shortly after prematurely giving a guy "the Boot" in the early stages of dating.

Unlike popular belief, men truly want love and want to give all their love in return - just like women supposedly do. Men are not throbbing

THE LOVING NATURE OF MEN - MISINTERPRETED

penises just seeking to penetrate every woman they can possibly find as most women seem to conclude. Men's feelings are very real! The reason some women can't seem to find so-called "Good Men," is simply because they keep making the same foolish mistakes, and the same bad choices, for the same thoughtless reasons when it comes to men.

As an example, guy meets girl; everything seems perfect: Mutual attraction, chemistry, etc. - are all powerful and present. This particular guy does not date too much, though, but possesses as much charm, tact, and "game" as the average guy. However, he's somewhat selective; he doesn't just aimlessly jump from relationship to relationship. His last relationship lasted a few years; and although it didn't *work-out*, he is the kind of guy who has his life "together" as far as his career and financial future is concerned. In addition, he is *in the market* for love and commitment - in the traditional sense. ("Commitment" *here refers, erroneously, to marriage as most of the inhabited World sees it. The validity of this premise will be dissected, examined, and discussed later.*)

As is obvious, this guy is not the "Player" type; so chances are, he only dates one woman at-a-time; he tries to make the best of a single situation. If it does not follow-through or work-out, he then moves-on to another possibility, etc. There are millions of men here in America, for example, who fits exactly into this criterion; their names may change, but their values remain the same. It's simple: they want *Love and Togetherness* just like many women claim to want.

As discussed earlier, some men naturally display or show signs of physical desire more readily than most women do, especially in the early stages of courtship. This does not mean the women would not be feeling the same strong desires also; they just conceal it better. Owing to the fact that he's not dating other women, this guy - in my example here - may be showing signs of being a bit anxious to get to the *physical*. He may not be aware of this; but women are especially perceptive when it comes to picking-up on these things in men. Instinctively, they just know this. Here-in lays the problem!

Generally, some women would perceive this to be a sign of *desperation* on his part; and as a result, would instantly become "turned-off," since, in the typical woman's mind, the conditioned response of "He seems desperate…. who *the hell* wants a desperate man?" is immediately brought to the forefront of her thinking. Consequently, she'll most probably lose all interest in this particular guy.

There are still others who are likely to assume that he must only be interested in the physical, and so presumed to have no other interest in them – otherwise. And once again, his fate would usually be the same.

Only a few women would exercise the discernment to give the situation a chance to evolve, in order to verify or negate their initial instinctive perception. You know of this latter type: they are the ones who are *unusually happy* and - most times - happily married.

On the flip side, consider a woman meeting a man who fits into the same above criterion except, instead of dating one woman at-a-time, he usually dates a few. For example, he dates somewhere in the range of 3 to 5 women at any given time. In other words, he's the "Player Type." This "Player Type" lifestyle affords him the ability to be much more relaxed and laid-back in the initial stages of dating. In contrast, the typical woman would erroneously perceive him to be "not so overly focused on the physical;" and as a result, would very likely further assume him to be more so interested in all the other things about her - other than *sex*. In other words, he would seem like the "perfect guy" to her.

Commonly, the typical woman would quickly and blindly *fall* for this second guy, only to soon find-out she was just an added *specimen* to his collection. We now know why "Players" continue to play. We meet these unhappy women every day. They'll say things such as the infamous, "Men Are Dogs!" Or "There are no good men *left* out there………..they are all taken!" Or my favorite: "Men just don't know what *the hell* they really want!" Remember: a bad choice is always directly related to its outcome! Therefore, if the outcome continues to be undesirable, it follows that we are simply making the same *bad* choices. The blame or responsibility is always *at home,* in the mirror, and no where else! It's that simple.

Once again, I find it rather amazing how much some women seem to always find it necessary to blame men for their own indiscretions. Women were simply endowed with natural instincts in order for them to recognize and respond aptly to the opposite sex (men). Recognizing *desire* in men does not mean - as some women would say - "I picked-up on his 'game,'..... and knew exactly what he was after... because *game recognize game!"* It simply means you're *normal!* Again: It simply means you're *normal!* That's it! That's all it is! It is precisely the way God designed you to work! Stop trying to be so smart that you keep *outsmarting* yourself! Men are not here with nothing else to do but to *deceive you!* If you keep expecting deceit from the men in your life, you'll have more than enough experiences of it to continually confirm your expectations.

Unfortunately, these are the type women who allow society, the media, their girl-friends, childhood influences, and many other related forces - especially so, deeply-instilled cultural codes - to sabotage their possibilities when it comes to men. They view displays of seeming premature or early physical desire in men, as being a *negative*; and mostly because, they continue to attempt to separate *the physical* from *the mental* and *the emotional* in relationships.

Women need to learn to identify with the fact that men are simply natural aggressors. They, in-turn, were designed to instinctively recognize and respond to this very aggression in men. The appropriate response is to first welcome the aggression as being *normal*; and to then, find a way to curtail it in the particular man – without negating interest. A woman *does not* have to give-in or fully reciprocate immediately - unless she really wants to. However, the fact that she correctly embraces it, and equally finds a way to curb or control it, in a positive way, will allow for his physical desires to build to incredible heights. This added anticipatory energy within him, will in-turn cause similar energies or feelings of mutual desire to be reciprocated within her. The appropriate unfolding of this process, can turn the courtship experience into a mutually-fulfilling, positive, mental chase, which, along with harmonious fundamentals and good verbal communication, can result in a mutually-explosive, emotional, mental, physical, and ultimately spiritual outcome between mates.

It is of paramount importance that women come to understand that what most men really want is to be allowed to *Love* them *in their own way*; and at-the-same-time, to be *Loved and Appreciated,* likewise. This should in no way, shape, or form be taken for granted - *ever!* The depth and longevity of every man-woman, monogamous, relationship heavily depends on its implementation.

# CHAPTER 5

# Marriage, The Institution of

For all that is said about uplifting the sacred *Institution of Marriage*, I can start here by citing statistical data which may serve to encourage or discourage any man or woman urgently seeking to engage in the *blissful ceremonial event*; but I wouldn't! Instead – being an individual centered mostly on favorable outcomes, positive results, and life-enriching consequences – I would rather examine the practicing intricacies which often render this worldly, so-called, sacred undertaking the hindrance rather than the "free road to happiness" as most of us vehemently believe

The keyword here is "worldly." Mankind has secularized God's intention for the union between a man and a woman into what I aptly call "A BIG JOKE;" and – get this – he actually expects it to work in his favor! To his dismay, the "BIG JOKE" is only on himself! He has allowed Pagan beliefs and practices to continually rob him of his rightful place as *Master of his own Destiny*. He continues to erroneously allow the external *worldly values* - as we know them - to dictate the purpose and outcome of his life, even though he has clear, supportable, evidence of generation after generation of unquestionable failure! In fact, present Man has faced so many failures, that generations before him have "flipped-the-script" to the point where many *past failures* are now falsely viewed as *successes* – as he aptly and conveniently sees them. For example, can someone please show me or tell me where the value exists in waging any *War* whatsoever? In my mind, the mere thought of *War* is primitive and grossly archaic - especially for a people who claim to be not only civilized, but "highly advanced!"

The fact is everything Man has so-called *created* with his hands - *outside*

MEN LOVE WOMEN.. WOMEN LOVE THEMSELVES

of himself, of course - clearly shows signs of an advanced civilization; however, *within* - deep within himself - he's *w a y* more primitive than ever were the *Cave Men!* This inner primordial tendency encompasses virtually his entire civilization, thus far; but for our purposes here, I will remain focused on the discussion at hand - although, unquestionably, it is this very *negligence of inner growth* which has been the cornerstone of most - if not *all* - of his lifelong generational failures and grievances.

One may ask the question, "Failure? What failure are you speaking of......are you blind?" But "The Blind" may just be the ones asking the questions. This "Failure," I am referring to, is the failure of productive, fulfilling, inter-personal, relationships and, specifically, marriages. Remember, as documented, God created the World, followed by Man, and then his companion - Woman. These three entities - the World (nature), Man, and Woman - were created by God to exist in delicate, hierarchal, harmony. Where there's *Harmony*, there's *Love*. In other words, *Love* only exists where *Harmony* exists and vice versa. Man has failed to successfully adhere to this basic three-point harmony structure between nature, himself, and his woman; therefore, he has been unable to experience true, sustainable, all-around, rightful, happiness in his life.

Furthermore, this hierarchy *must* not only be adhered to for man to live in true harmony with himself, his woman, and nature, but also for him to live in true harmony with everyone and everything else around him on this planet and in the entire Universe, as a whole. In terms of man and his correlation to his brothers and sisters – which is an absolute necessity for him – *all of life encompasses relationships.*

According to the Scriptures and, to some extent, modern Science, the World (nature) was first created. This suggests that for all we do, *we must* first accept and respect the laws of nature. Unknown to man, he has actually partially - though not fully - held fast to these laws to some degree. When we look at the many "Wonders of the World" in every facet of life, for example, we may erroneously conclude that man has actually outdone himself; and so, can rightfully call himself *Great!* However, this

*P "Nalagy" Browne*

83

is not so! This seeming greatness of Mankind is actually God's creative power working through him. Every known invention or creation in life, started with a sustained thought, followed by the unwavering desire and steadfast longing to realize it (called *Intention* or *True Faith*). When any man insistently engages nature, the Universe, and therefore God, in this way, he instantly summons the creative powers of God (the Universe) into motion. Soon people, circumstances, and events start presenting themselves to him in such a way that, in short duration, his unyielding thoughts become *his reality*. Therefore, in this regard, *Man* is simply the endless "Conduit of Possibilities" through which God (Universal Intelligence) continues his/its never-ending creative work. This is Universal Law!

However, for the most part, man has failed to understand his relationship to the above process; and so, never quite realizes how these forces work in his life. Given his material success, he blindly tries to apply his self-serving, egotistical, misunderstandings of himself to his personal love life. In that, he tries to make it whatever he wills. The problem here is, although God (Universal Intelligence) gives him some level of free-will to access creation, to some degree - whether he believes there's a God or not - without the true knowledge and clear understanding of himself, his relationship to nature, his woman, and every other being through *The Unselfish Respect and Appreciation He Holds For His Own Existence* (what I term "Self Love"), he is doomed to experience continual chaos in every area of his life - and for the most part, he has! Look around! Remember, no amount of material possession brings *Love* and *Happiness* into anyone's life! Material possessions – especially money – only serve to bring to the surface and correspondingly amplify *whatever* it is that we have identified with already. Thus, *Happiness* can only be attained through rigorously recognizing and adhering to God's will (The existing, never-changing laws of the Universe); and is, in itself, unrelated to material creative access in every way. For example, a lot of "what" has been created - thus far - can be categorized under the heading of "weaponry," which only serves to encourage war and globalize *chaos*, and will ultimately lead to Man's *self-*

*destruction* in the final analysis.

*Love,* and *Love* alone, is the "glue" which *binds* nature with mankind. Therefore, the harmonious bond between nature and Man is - and always has been and will forever continue to be - *Love* it self. This simply means that Man, himself, is connected to nature and therefore, cannot in any way be disconnected from it. So, as it stands, Man can only feel and experience true unconditional *Love* - *the only Love there is* - for himself and his woman, and vice versa, through *his awareness* of the laws of nature already established by God (The Universe), and remains fully available to him by virtue of his existence. As long as he adheres to these laws, *Happiness* is inevitable; if he doesn't – you know the drill! In other words, he better *Recognize!*

Man's main dilemma in life rests in the fact that he had been taught from childhood that *Love* is something he should be looking for "outside of himself;" and so, his mindset often hovers around the thought of, "How can I use what I have to get what I want?" As a result, all that he has presumably "created," have been used primarily for the purpose of attracting and possibly keeping or securing this *Love* and *Happiness* he constantly seeks - since this *thing* he craves most can only be found *out-there* somewhere. This seemingly simple misunderstanding has been the underlying source of all of his *Love* and *Happiness* related problems thus far.

To understand the profound effects of this deeply embedded, self-alienating, belief system we must first examine its origin. Many Christian-based religious persuasions and their corresponding governmental and social structures - whether deliberate or otherwise - lead their congregation (and therefore, their related communities) to uphold the belief system which says that *God* and *Love* are entities which exist *outside* of the individual. In other words, they teach of *separation from God,* to be the norm for mankind, unless he "gives his soul to God by first repenting his sins, and then asking God (Jesus) to enter into his or her heart." Whether seen as truth or fiction is left to individual belief, and will not be discussed here. Nonetheless, since our recognition of *God* and *Love* sparks the same emotions within us, this belief system has left the average Man scrambling to fill the resulting *God-Love* void he feels deep within himself. This situation, in-turn, leads him to naturally abandon or, for lack of a better term, completely neglect his "Upper-Self," which is that part of his *being* receptive to Godlike recognition and perception, and to instead, cling steadfastly to his "Lower-Self," which is that part of his *being* driven and mastered by none other than his self-serving *Ego*. This *Ego* of Man has proven to be more destructive than you can possibly imagine!

In addition to the preceding personal dilemma, just about everything in our society, as we know it, that which we have been reared to see and accept as *normal,* also summons and encourages this very *Ego* of ours - further inflicting even more self-destructive dominion over our lives. By this I mean, *everything in control:* All the disciplines and principles of our government; the Media – all Media; all that we as humans become subjected to on a daily basis - from all directions; the laws; the way the laws are enforced; the whole idea that we must have *this* and we need to have *that,* in place, because humans are naturally *bad*; etc The endless list of rules, regulations, and necessary directives goes on and on and on.

So what are we left with? We're left with a deep-rooted, *Ego-driven, Institution* guiding our lives, which taught us - and continues to teach us since we were babies - how much we *want* to do "Bad Things" to each other; how much we naturally desire to *hurt* and *undermine* one another. It's just something we *must* accept as being the truth about ourselves! As a direct result, we typically grow-up thinking everything in life requires irrefutable *Competition*. Life involves an endless battle that we *must* endure against our *Brothers* and *Sisters* in order to "get what's rightfully ours - if we're lucky." Supposedly, all this is absolutely necessary if our ultimate desire, in this life, is to "win" and "not lose" to someone else - that is, if we hope to eventually be "Somebody" someday!

You're probably wondering, "How is all this remotely related to the topic of discussion?" So, to satisfy your expected curiosity, let me jump to the *punch-line.* You see, so many past generations have been subjected to the foregoing forces, and the subsequent corresponding habitual mindset has become so deeply engraved into our subconscious, that most of us (including all politicians, law makers and enforcers, all religious bodies, the media, all other governmental bodies, etc) accept it as our *Unquestionable Reality*! Every time we turn-on the "Idiot Box" (the TV) or read the morning newspaper, we get confirmed proof of this so-called "Truth!" Even the songs on the radio tell the same misleading stories - clearly revealing the true fabric of our resulting *Ego-driven* minds, the false values we have collectively bought into as our own. In fact, the very Constitution of The United States - in my opinion - had been written and adhered-to from this very same egotistical perspective. However, this is not where it ends!

Most of us further engross ourselves into even more profound mental and emotional turmoil, when we passively allow the preceding mindset to become what we uphold and defend all-the-way from childhood to our graves; our lifelong habitual ways of being and acting. With such a prevailing self-view, it has become seemingly natural for us to approach our personal, love and/or marriage lives from this very same perspective. After-all, if the *Ego* is in the driver's seat, it follows that we *must* go wherever it takes us. This is the fertile soil in which the common seeds of relationship turmoil typically germinate and allowed to violently grow out of control! Can you now see how this could possibly be the main underlying reason for the unusually high relationship and marriage dissolution rate in our society? Maybe not....so let's dig a little deeper.

Just as in the consumer market, we're constantly directed *how* to shop, *where* to shop, *when* to shop, *what* to buy, and *where* and *who* to buy from, we're driven by this very same system which also dictates what's "valuable" and what's "not valuable" in our own personal relationships. These additional *Drivers* are primarily put in place by mega, retail-driven, corporations that spend billions and billions of dollars each year on perfecting consumer-targeted *Psychological Brainwash or Programming* and endless *Ego-Targeted* gimmicks, specifically designed to spark and, for-the-most-part, *secure* huge profits, all at the expense of keeping the masses *living like sheep!*

Crazy as it may seem, the preceding practices are not in any way new; they have been in place for hundreds of years. What has happened, though, is that, with time, they have simply become more profoundly adept at inflicting their brainwash tactics. So now, when they "pull our strings" we instantly react like *trained puppets* - predictably thinking and doing exactly what's expected of us.

With these forces in-place, relationships and marriages have become a direct by-product of this *Commercial Brainwash Anarchy*; praying on the physically weaker, but boosted by our social and economic system to effectively act as the emotionally stronger sex. In this way, they are able to effectively control women by preying on their emotions, which, by the way, are also mastered and controlled by the very same self-serving *Ego* - once again; and so, are able to indirectly control the more naturally logical, less directly influenced, men. This subliminal control base has been the death-nail which continually seals the coffin of destruction for many, many, many, many, many marriages - long, long, long, before the actual weddings take place!

Most men would passively tell you, "The wedding is always about the Bride..... It's her day to be the Princess she learned and dreamed about way back when she was a kid." Typically, the man's purpose is commonly resigned to the buying of a ridiculously expensive engagement ring; in most cases, paying for the entire wedding, since it's "Her Day;" and then, just showing-up to say "I do" however many times, as necessary, to give her-her most revered moment. These men are not *getting-it!* They are not seeing that this dismissive outlook on life is the main reason why their marriages are in the disorder they're in from the *get-go!*

Recognize that the worldly reason for this "wedding" referred to above, is the predictable outcome of a subconsciously-staged, deeply-embedded, preconditioned, desire instilled in women in the early years of childhood, carrying a predetermined time-coding constraint. The typical male finds himself with the typical female, who is approaching 30 yrs old, and now suddenly *on the warpath* for this "thing" called *marriage* – regardless of the present compatibility level in their relationship.

Also understand that the disciplines and principles set forth by God (naturally and inherently instilled in our psyche) in order for the pending union to possibly and effectively "work," are normally not in place in the typical situation. Put simply, this means that the present relationship is not commonly based on any of the individual's first *unselfishly* loving themselves, and so would correspondingly possess the needed capacity to truly respect and appreciate (Love) the other for who they are at the very core of their being. I know this may sound like a group of well chosen words put together without real-life meaning to some of us; however, the reality is, without this unselfish respect and appreciation, first for *self*, to the point of overflowing in order to then include the other individual, the marriage and hope for happiness as a result of it – being her most revered desire – would remain nothing more than a wish that never-ever comes to true fruition.

The "…time-coding constraint" mentioned above, refers to the fact that there's an unwritten law in our society, which says: "If a woman is not married by the time she's 30 years old, things are not looking very good for her – future-wise. However, if by age 40 this situation has not been rectified, she has failed miserably as a woman!" Our society now secretly, or in reference, frowns on her as an *Incurable Failure*; she is now viewed as being "Useless," "Undesirable" or "Unwanted" for marriage by any man. The typical woman, in-turn, believes this *False Truth* as a result of her deeply-embedded, pagan-driven, childhood-instilled cultural coding; and consequently, it frequently becomes her *Enduring Reality*.

To justify the importance of the above urgency, our society has come-up with a host of thoughtless reasoning that women regurgitate like sick puppies. *They range from*, "My biological clock is ticking….I want to have kids….but I am not having kids out of wedlock……..I wasn't raised that way!" *All the way to*: "My parents are getting older…they want to see me married before they die." "Why should he buy the Cow, when he can get the milk for free?" "He doesn't want to make a commitment to me.....he's probably searching for something better out-there!" And the list goes on and on.

Many of you are probably sitting there in awe, trying to figure-out where the fault lies in any of the foregoing, commonly-used statements. Ok! While you're there trying to find a way to get your lower jaw up off the floor, understand that nothing is specifically wrong with making any of the foregoing statements; it's the *Driver* behind the 'making' of such statements which cradles the self-demeaning predicament. These women have passively allowed forces *outside of themselves* (unrelated to their unique, personal lives and relationships) to regulate the reality of what actually transpires *within* their lives and relationships.

We *must* come to terms with the fact that no human can 'build' a *natural tree*, for example. This requires a process put in place my nature - and nature alone. Every known *natural tree* on the face of this earth started the process of its growth with a seed, which germinated and first grew into a small plant. This small plant later became a grown, mature, tree only with time. In addition, this grown, mature, tree had to be cared-for and nurtured in order to become the strong tree it finally turned-out to be.

We can somehow equate the preceding *natural tree* growth process to the necessity involved in building lifelong relationships; there are *no* short-cuts, and there are *no* exceptions to this general rule – irrespective of what age group you happen to be in. You don't have the "right," by of virtue of being a woman, to *deserve* a great relationship and marriage, and to live "Happily Ever After" as the Fairy Tale goes. You don't just *show-up* - being pretty - and *happiness* just falls into your lap like magic! Every relationship requires *work* in the form of *nurturing, self-growth,* and *unselfish compromise* – unless you really want to be in this relationship by and with yourself!

Men are not blameless, though, in allowing the preceding mindset to soar out of control like a derailed, high-speed, run-away train. Passively, they have bought into this type thinking on the receiving end, as a result of a male-directed systemized form of mental programming, which indirectly presents itself through the very same "Happily Ever After" fairy tale fantasy.

When the *Power* to be men is taken away from or not upheld by men, the results can never-ever paint a pretty picture - as is all so obvious in our society today. Basically, we are at a place where, on a subconscious level, most men deeply believe they're supposed to somehow meet women "wherever they are." In other words, the average man willingly and forcibly alters *whoever* he really is, at the core, in an attempt to fit-into *whatever* he thinks the particular woman is, expects, or wants him to be - irrespective of her up-bringing, value system, and so on. She is supposedly "Perfect" in his eyes and mind. To him, this is the only road to "True Happiness" in his life, in his relationships, and especially so, in his marriage. Such men have voluntarily accepted *death of Self*, without consciously realizing it! I see this as the prevailing predicament men typically find themselves in here in America, and, for that matter, in any other territory or country where the American way of life is upheld and practiced. The women *expect it;* the men *act it out;* and *true happiness* is forever forfeited - on both sides - as the end result.

As mentioned above, the road to *happiness* in any relationship "... requires *work* in the form of *nurturing, self-growth* and *unselfish compromise.*" These three life-enriching characteristics can be naturally and easily accomplished, if only we were able to permanently dismiss the seeming *Power* and *Control* our self-serving *Egos* exert over our lives.

Understand that your Ego - if left unchecked - can turn out to be your greatest adversary. It is what tells you "You *must win* at all cost... to anyone and everyone else!" "You *must* get what you think you *must have,* and it is *absolutely necessary* to step-on or undermine others to do so!" "If you let him/her win, then he'll/she'll think he/she has something over you, and you can't *live* with that!" It is what tells you the word "compromise" means "your way only," since *it's all about you* (in the case of women – generally)! It is what leads us to believe that *acts of selfishness,* on our part, mean self-preservation, in a selfless way, but when subjected to the same acts on the receiving end, they suddenly take-up their true *egotistical* meanings. It is what leads us to misuse the word "Pride;" to think it somehow means "self-respect" - even-though the Bible clearly speaks-out against getting caught-up in its vicious claws. I only comprehend the word "Pride" to represent egotism, arrogance, self-importance, self-righteousness, vanity, conceit, pre-eminence, self-interest, and *pure* selfishness – all of which, individually and collectively, shuts-off the very *essence of life* for anyone who chooses to practice emulating any of them. I consider the only rightful competition to be the competition one conducts *with* oneself on the path to continual self-improvement, as in, *striving to be better than you were yesterday – everyday!* As Dr. Wayne W. Dyer puts it while speaking on this sentiment:

"...At every single moment of your life, you have the choice to either be a *Host to God* or a *Hostage to your Ego....*"

The choice is *always* yours!

As an aside: Notice carefully that I didn't assert "...the competition one conducts *against* oneself.." The mere thought of viewing any competition as being *against* anyone or anything - including yourself - actually works against or literally *weakens* the individual harboring and participating in such power-dissipating practices.

Once again: When the *Power* to be men is taken away from or not upheld by men, the results can never-ever paint a pretty picture. It is fact that a man can *only* be a man when he has the *Power* to do so. This *Power* needs to be built-up and re-assured within him every day; especially so, by his woman. The Bible outlines this to be one of the primary reasons why God decided to put her in his life. Simply put, he needs her support in order to be the rightful, *Powerful,* man God intended him to be. The blunder is, women sometimes cannot seem to comprehend (mainly as a result of our Ego-driven, self-confusing, society) that by encouraging and embracing their Man's *Power,* they too would in-turn be *empowered* to be the rightful, *Powerful,* women God intended them to be. There is a purposeful reason why God used a rib of Man to create Woman: She is designed to be his *Support* and Him her *Protector;* not by *force,* but by *virtue.* Also, a Man can live without his rib, but his rib cannot live without him.

As it stands, a woman naturally gets her own *Power* through supporting or empowering her man. It's that simple! If she fails or refuses to support and embrace his *Power*, she loses her own *Power*; and consequently, the relationship or marriage usually suffers demise. Now you know why the divorce rate in our society has been skyrocketing out of control; the women are simply not providing the necessary support their men need. This "demise," though, does not necessarily mean break-up, separation, or even divorce. There are hundreds of thousands - even millions - of what I refer to as "Dead Marriages" out there, where couples are just "going through the motion" for many, many years in *Power-Draining* rather than *Power-Evolving* relationships.

On the flip side, some men really have no *Power* for their women to embrace! This is very real! This fact remains a mostly unaddressed issue in our society; and simply because, some men are reared to approach their lives from a commonly unaware, *Powerless*, "I am the victim," standpoint - giving-up their own *Power* to the worldly belief system which says, "The woman is the Boss!" Also, if the particular woman happens to *bring home* more money than the man or husband, in question, this gives her the right to be "The Boss-to-the-2nd Power!" In his mind, he cannot remotely claim to be a "Real Man," since his significance as such - in accordance with the prevailing *Ego-driven, Fear-based, societal* directive - only lies in him being the dominant provider in the marriage. If he's not, he evidently "does not wear the pants in the marriage" as most would judge. Accordingly, this means his role as the Man in the marriage relationship, would be understandably relinquished to his woman. This is the *nonsense* traditional cultural practices have taught him to believe and to embrace!

This *Power*, endowed by God, rests deep inside every man (and woman). All he has to do is reach within and summon it into practical existence. On a subconscious level, every man knows this; he simply continually ignores or misinterprets the call. Also, no gender *should* be seen as "The Boss" in any relationship. Men and women were designed, by our creator, to play specific roles which delicately complement and synchronize with each other in a harmoniously-balanced, mutually-gratifying, way - continually adding fulfilling nurturing energy to the particular relationship. No woman is remotely intended to play the role of a man in any relationship or marriage. By the same token, no man is remotely designed to play the role of a woman.

Let's take a closer look at this *Power* I keep referencing in the last few paragraphs. Understand that *everything* is about *Power!* This *Power*, though, has nothing to do with our present - soon to be previous - understanding of the term. As mentioned earlier, this *Power* is only from *within*. Thus, it can only be accessed through cultivating personal control on the premise of *Self - from within*; and not "to be controlled," on the premise of the *Ego - from without*. In other words, this *Power* is purely *Spiritual*; and as such, can *only* be accessed and attained by giving *Self* (your *Spiritual Self*) the control - effectively dismissing control by your *Ego*. And further, the only way to truly appreciate and develop this *Power*, is through *being of service* (empowering) to others.

Accordingly, we are all *One* in *Spirit*; so the *Power* of each, only adds to the overall *Power* of the whole. Therefore, in this *Power-evolving* Universe, we can only rightfully get what we want and be what we want to be when we possess the necessary *Power* to do so. Charles F. Haanel, puts it nicely in his book, *The Master Key System*, written in 1912:

"...when Man awakens to the *Truth*, and affirms his Oneness with all life, he finds that he takes-on the *clear eye*, the elastic step, the vigor of youth; he finds that he has discovered the source of *All Power*......and this *Power* is (only) *Spiritual Power*, and this *Spiritual Power* is the *Power* which lies at the heart of all things; it is *The Soul of the Universe.....*"

Feelings of *God, Love*, and true *Power* are one and the same. Therefore, our true feelings related to *God*, are always feelings of *Love*; and our true feelings of *Love*, are the only real positive *Power* we as humans possess (True *Faith* or *Intention* is simply this *Power* in *Mental* and *Spiritual* action - directed with steadfast desire and purpose). This *Power*, therefore, is *an emission*; a *giving*; a *radiation* - never an *expectation*. It's not what we feel "coming-in," but what we feel "coming back" to us as a result of what we *radiate*. Everything else we refer to as *Power* is purely *Ego-based* (the desire *to get,* instead of the desire *to give*) which is, as mentioned above, *Power-Draining,* rather than *Power-Evolving*.

In our society and in our World today, because of generation upon generation of misuse, we have embraced an erroneous viewpoint of this personal *Power*. In general, when we hear the word *Power* being used, the first thing that typically comes to mind is "Necessary control of or by others." This is the only relationship we seem to know and uphold thus far. Often, we only relate *Power* to leadership figures, in terms of Presidents, the government, etc; and to anyone else who is in a position of influence or control, such as pastors, our bosses at work, and so on. I am suggesting that you re-evaluate your viewpoint of *Power*. Understand that if these individuals or figures are not empowering you to be the best "you" that "you" can be, or helping you to realize and use your own *Power* for good, then they are actually exploiting your *Power* for selfish means only!

This remains the all-too-obvious guiding principle of all but a few so-called leaders throughout our inhabited World. Their platform is clearly *Ego-Based,* for them, and *Power-Draining* for you. Know this! The idea is, as long as they can keep you ignorant of your own *Power,* your own personal self-control and self-worth, they are able to keep you weak; and as long as you are weak, you will continue to recognize them as your source of *Power;* you will continue to see them as being *significant* to your life; you will continue to dream or "pay" for what I call "False Hope." The only true purpose of *Leadership* (all forms of *Leadership)* is to empower others for unselfish motives. In my mind, no other purpose or motive for leadership makes sense!

In light of the above generational hereditary understanding of personal *Power,* here again, we as humans try to apply what we grasp as "Truth to the World," and apply it to our personal lives, on the premise that we need to "control others" in order to "show" or validate our own *Power,* which we loosely relate to *Love,* in a self-confusing way. Most of us open-handedly accept this self-view as absolutely necessary – until now; never seeming to grasp that our *Power* relationship to *Love* can never be *control of and over others,* but rather, *control of and over ourselves.*

Just as we are kept weak by those we choose to call our *Leaders,* we instinctively think this is what we need to do to keep or to secure the person we want or believe we *must have* in our lives. Every day we continually hear of stories concerning couples - married or otherwise - involved in what we commonly refer to as "Power-Struggles" in their relationships; invariably leading to break-up or divorce. We also hear, see, and read the viewpoints of far-too-many doctors, therapist, authors and other "worldly" authorities, *rant and rave* on the issues, while assigning endless tags and reasoning for the dilemma - none of which, in my opinion, addresses the truly sources of the ongoing problems.

*Let it be known*: There are not such things as true "Power-Struggles" in relationships or marriages! If *God* is *Love,* and *Love* is *Power,* how could there ever be any "battle" or "struggle" on any such grounds? It's simply not possible! What these couples go-through are "Ego-Struggles" or "Ego-Battles;" never "Power-Struggles." They are experiencing tribulations *within* their relationships or marriages, based on or driven by external forces and values (from *without*), which they have allowed to influence their own actions; and as such, are completely unrelated to *God, Love,* and *True Power* in every sense. If everything they see, hear, understand, believe, and apply to their lives - whether deliberate or otherwise – is *Ego-Based,* then their relationships and/or marriages must also be *Ego-Based.* Remember, an *Ego-Based* relationship or marriage faces inevitable self-destruction.

Also, under this very realm, sometimes women, because of what seems to be their traditionally twisted understanding of workable life processes and values, choose to somehow view all of their relationships (with the opposite gender) as volatile, but their impending marriages as to be permanent. Unlike popular belief, if one cannot or chooses not to include a sense of the possibility of permanence in every relationship one finds oneself in, prior to any marriage, it is virtually impossible for one to feel or practice any true sense of permanence thereafter or during any marriage. Life does not turn on and off like light switches.

I do know that far too many of us are reared to believe that with "God's blessings and approval" during the marriage ceremony, a miraculous bond or sense of oneness will somehow suddenly and magically appear between couples. Let me humbly apologize, in advance, for being the bearer of *bad* news. This approach has never worked and probably never would in the future! Put simply, what we practice becomes habit, and habits are difficult and most times, impossible to break for most of us. We can pretend and force the issue for a short time; but very soon, we'll unquestionably return to our ingrained patterns or practicing habits.

This also applies to the common practice of fervently attempting to "change" the other individual in the particular marriage. Don't ever think you're so special that you can somehow suddenly *change* a lifelong habit in another simply because you're now married to them. You can only effect change through encouragement; you cannot effect change through force. The particular person has got to want to make the *change* (whatever it may be), and *force* only creates and encourages more resistance to this requested or desired change.

All too often, I see far too many situations where, in an attempt to please the other, one person puts-up a façade - forcefully displaying a pretense of the desired or requested change that was asked of or forced upon them. This sham can only last but for so long! And typically, when the *curtains of pretense* are finally lifted, deep feelings of resentment, coupled with corresponding feelings of blame and deceit, predictably comes to the surface. Then, on both sides, the validity of the other's Love and integrity suddenly become *Judge* and *Jury.*

Many of us find ourselves in the above dilemma, and especially so after marriage. Simply put, we live in a society which tells us, in a nut shell, and mostly from a woman's perspective, that only marriages are important; our relationships are always secondary. Why? Because (and this is where

I am convinced that the underlying problem rests) men are reared to see themselves as "nothing" without a woman, whereas women are raised to see themselves as "useless" without marriage! Therefore, the issues in a relationship really don't ever need to be addressed until after "The goose gets the golden egg" (marriage), since, then, they would suddenly become "One," and it's now her cue to finally "Fix him" to meet her requirements!

The objective is to just go-ahead and get married, and by an act of faith or divine intervention, the relationship will somehow naturally take care of itself. And if it doesn't, the practicing directive is to just "keep-on trying *the marriage thing,* and someday, you'll hopefully find a marriage that will work for you..... There is absolutely nothing to be gained in valuing relationships; what you *should* always be looking for is marriage....if you're a woman and you're over 30!" In other words, you should go-ahead and make marriage your main objective; after the fact, you can then check to see if the "man you got" is who you really wanted to share the rest of your life with!

It is obvious here that the man in the marriage is typically seen as an object or a tool to be used to satisfy a seeming "greater ambition" staged by his woman, which more often than not has absolutely nothing to do with him as a person. In other words, he is commonly viewed as a pet animal, for example, which is to be trained to act and react in whatever ways his woman – now his wife – expects of him

Ok, let's try to make some kind of sense out of this preposterous nonsense! If when it gets right down to it a marriage is simply an official declaration of *a relationship* (where the government and the church (God) become involved), doesn't it make logical sense that the relationship "should be," and "is," of utmost importance to and especially prior to the marriage? And if this is indeed so, that the marriage can and will naturally stand a fighting chance to take care of itself? This is the kind of blind, flip-flopped, twisted reality we have guiding our lives every day - all in the name of Tradition, or what I like to refer to as *blind, foolish, ignorance!* The relationship is absolutely everything! Nothing else really matters! If both parties can't keep that together, they should do each other a huge favor and simply part ways. Marriage does not *fix* anything! Once again: Marriage does not *fix* anything! It is not going to somehow make you now accept the things you've always deeply disliked about him or her; it only *amplifies* them. Are you getting this? Nor will marriage magically make you now start feeling a deeper, more profound sense of *Love and Affection* towards that other person, simply because you now finally "got what you've always wanted!" It's all an illusion! The indispensable value and cultivation of the particular relationship, is the only remotely viable preparation for a workable marriage.

More often than not, though, men have allow women – urgently seeking to experience their externally-orchestrated "Princess Moment" – to direct their lives *down* this very path; jumping into premature, unequally yoked marriages from relationships that hold less chances of remaining intact than a thatched shed in the direct path of a category four hurricane. Good luck!

The average couple would generally be thinking some version of the following: "Ok, if both of us are spending time together, sleeping together and enjoying it," for a pre-determined length of time - typically set and enforced by the woman and driven, once again, by the rules of our society, through the seeming undeniable directive called *Tradition* - "we might-as-well go ahead and tie the knot; we're not getting any younger you know!" This is usually the entire depth of the decision.

Just think, when we're in the process of building a house or buying a new home, we carefully choose the neighborhood, the *best* schools for our kids, appropriate size house, included interior furnishings, color schemes, landscaping - everything! Also, when we set-out to purchase a new vehicle, for example, we generally surf the internet for consumer satisfactory reports; we go from dealership to dealership to test drive, touch, smell, and thoroughly explore different makes and models; and most times, we may even venture to haggle for a better deal in terms of pricing, optional equipment, etc. However, when it comes to our own person, it is so-so sad how much we blindly and haphazardly allow our lives to drift on the ocean of time, like rudderless ships - sails ripped to threads - uncontrollably tossed into whatever direction our childhood-conditioned tide of life takes us - all in the senseless, outmoded, bewildering name of *Tradition*.

## Fear and the Ego

Then there's this thing called *Fear* which most of us openly embrace, giving it total precedence over our marriages (our relationships) and our entire lives as a whole. Put simply, we tend to collectively recognize and accept the dominant emotion of *Fear* to be a *normal* and *necessary* part of living. Just in case you're unaware, all forms of worry and stress are derived from the mental harboring of fearful thoughts. This corresponds to the fact that all sickness and disease, which typically manifest as result of *stress*, are indeed direct by-products of *Fear* also.

As humans, the common practice of embracing or continually harboring the emotion of *Fear* is equivalent to voluntarily inviting physical death while still fervently wanting to continue to live! I know this comparison sounds ridiculous - and it is - but this is exactly what most of us subconsciously put ourselves through every single day! Please understand that *Fear* is a direct adjunct of your Ego. Therefore, if you're being repeatedly bombarded with fearful thoughts, it's a tell-tale sign that your *Ego* is in *full control* of your psyche, and *pain* and *sorrow* are on *the express train* into your life - if not there already.

All that we *Fear* derive from our own habitual, subconsciously-held, conditioning much like the addictive "taste" we develop for the "bad foods" most of us incessantly ingest into our bodies, even though we may be quite aware of the unfathomable damage they can and will cause. Most , deliberately ignoring the fact that these habits can indeed be easily altered or changed by practicing and developing new ones; those proven to be more *pro-life*, instead of *pro-death*.

We often act as if we have no self-control - whatsoever! Basically, most of us fervently believe it's an absolute requirement to mimic everyone else. It is what necessitates "being normal" or "fitting-in to the scheme of things" to most of us. In that, we allow ourselves to passively succumb to "whatever," feeling an artificial sense of contentment as we "join-the-line;" inwardly concluding "This must be what life is all about!" Remember: If you're not embracing life, you are - without question - embracing death! It is precisely the reason why we were all given *Freedom of Choice* by our Creator. You simply cannot be on the fence with this one, you *must* make a choice! And unknown to most, we all have - the fruits of which are forever projected on the screens of our lives in the favorable or unfavorable circumstances we find ourselves in everyday. As author James Allen puts it:

"Circumstance does not make the man (or woman); it reveals him to himself!"

Whatever you're experiencing or have experienced in your life - good or bad - is solely as a consequent of your own doing; the decisions you have made and correspondingly acted upon - whether they be mental or physical. Thoughts, themselves, have proven to be a form of mental action. To this end, we must all take full responsibility and ownership for all that we encounter, instead of passing the blame unto someone or something else. Our circumstances only serve as a feed-back mechanism to the path we have chosen; continually revealing to us, the fruits or results of the decisions we've made. There is no other valid explanation to this!

*Fear*, itself, is not only a direct adjunct of the Ego; it's more like its Siamese twin. In that, the same forces that spark and support egotistical control over an individual, also encourage the harboring of *Fear* (fearful thoughts) in that same individual. The Ego instills its harm through doubt; and doubt blossoms into debilitating Fear. In other words, your *Ego* gives the harboring of *Fear* credence, and the *Fear* you're harboring, gives your *Ego* full dominion over you! Understand that as long as you're living in *Fear*, you are living *outside* of yourself. This means, you have made the choice to live in pure unadulterated weakness or *Powerlessness!* Once again, true *Power* is living from *within*; true *weakness* (*Fear*) is living from *without!*

Your *Ego* is the primary driving force, through which your own internal dialogue becomes continually bombarded with an endless stream of fear-infused thoughts, which may include, for example, "Hey, there is a great possibility I might be losing something....I should always expect this!" "I've got to be careful! ... Chances are someone - somewhere - is probably planning to do something awful to me!" "I believe my husband, wife, neighbor, co-worker, the gas station attendant, my boss, brother's wife, sister's husband, etc – are all trying to make my life miserable!" "I have no other choice but to keep the people I supervise weak; if I don't, they'll realize I am a *fake*; I can't have that! Therefore, I must keep them *worried* in order for me to look good – after-all, I am the Boss and that's what Bosses do......I am simply doing my job!" "I am the most important person here! I demand to be praised by everyone else; I simply deserve it!" Or "Everyone is better than I am; I have no value! I don't believe I even deserve to continue living; what's the use?" And this type internal dialogue of fear-based powerlessness, keeps generating and generating to the point where it has created on-going, seemingly-progressive World cultures: pride-worthy curriculums in schools and universities; booming businesses; best-selling authors; so-called, powerful Leadership in politics, religion, etc; thriving careers in medicine, law, entertainment and most Media. And the list goes on and on.

This *Fear*, along with its Siamese twin, the *Ego* has had such profound far-reaching effects in our society and world, that they remain the on-going underlying cause behind all wars; all forms of corruption in government and otherwise; all terrorism; all crime; all marital abuse and conflicts in relationships and marriages; the underlying driver behind the establishment and implementation of *The Institution of Marriage*; the sole cause of all divorces and "Dead Marriages." This list is inexhaustible! As long as anyone is experiencing *pain* and *sorrow*, of any kind, it's always *Fear* and the *Ego* at work in some form or another. Believe this!

Most would readily dismiss this as the way it was, is, and always would be; therefore, to most, the possibility of a more positive outlook and experience in life seems to only represent wishful, utopia-type thinking. This remains the popular notion; and primarily because, it has been deeply cemented into most of us (from childhood that is) how necessary and commendable it is to *Fear* God. Consequently, we have consciously joined *God* with the profoundly weakening emotion, *Fear,* which we keep harboring and defending. The direct result of this is to create a society - and it has - based in religion, where *Fear* runs everything! As it follows, when we perceive *God,* we also perceive *Love;* so, as a direct consequence of all this, most have foolishly completed the triangle by consciously and subconsciously amalgamating *God* with *Love* and *Fear,* instead of *God* with *Love* and personal *Power* - as intended by our Creator.

To this end, the standing edict when applied to marriages and relationships becomes, "If I love someone, it's necessary for me to *Fear* something! I've got to protect myself, since my loving him/her makes me vulnerable to being hurt." "Should I say how I truly feel? It can and may be used against me – you know? Ok, maybe I'll just not say how I feel....If I do he/she may break-up with me and break my heart. I must always worry about the possibility of this in every relationship." "I need *a guarantee* that ensures he/she can't just simply walk-away from this relationship." Or "let me *dig* as deeply as I can to find something - somewhere - in this relationship to *worry about;* it's just me being normal and realistic."

By the same token, the *Egotistical* side may be saying things such as, for example,

"I will not answer or return his calls – for a while – just to see how much he *Loves* me!.......I feel so much more in-control when I make him/her sweat a little!" "Even if I am wrong, I can't apologize, because that shows *weakness* and, as a man, I can't show this.....she needs to just get-over it!" "He told me how he felt about me *too soon*...........this means he must be desperate............He's too *weak* for me!" "I believe he wants to *dump me*...I'll act as if I don't care and *dump him* first, so I can be the one who *wins* (ended it)!" "In the beginning he was very *cold-hearted* towards me; he never returned the Love I was giving. Now that he claims to Love and need me......I'll put him through the same insecurity and heartache that I went through!"

It is *Fear* and *Ego* that would drive any individual to think and act in any of the above ways; and it is this same *Fear* and *Ego* that would encourage one person to break-up with or hurt another, on the same grounds. But all this would only make it clearly evident that they got together, in the first place, on the grounds of *Fear* and *Ego*.

Guy meets girl, for example. Guy satisfies her *Ego* (or vice-versa) by telling her whatever she needs to hear, in-accordance with her prior conditioning, to *temporarily* dismiss her *Fears*, and a relationship which may eventually lead to marriage, begins. The reason I used the word *"temporarily"* here, is simply because the dismissal of *Ego-based Fear* can only be temporary! As long as we're living our lives based in *Fear* and *Ego* - as sure as the sun will rise tomorrow - the *Fear* is bound to come back! Guaranteed, it's coming back! The *Ego* is your assurance of its return.

The return of this *Ego*-based *Fear*, becomes evident in the constant internal strife, including arguments and other forms of verbal and sometimes physical abuse, typically present in a significant number of what I refer to as "Seasoned Marriages" (after 3 to 5 years of marriage) in our society. These conflicts commonly stem from existing, pent-up, internal discontentment in some form or another. The discontentment itself, more often than not, stemming from some level of dissatisfaction or some sort of unmet expectation on the *Ego-Fear* platform. As a result, couples typically encounter repeated "Ego-Struggles" or, more accurately, *Fear-Ego* trade-offs, which continually wreak havoc on their relationships and marriages.

The usual picture of what transpires is, for example, a couple gets married, and this *Fear-Ego* trade-off carries-on for a number of years, literally 'Killing' any likelihood of true sustained intimacy or respect or appreciation or anything else for that matter. Then, the situation soon matures itself into a couple, with 1 to 3 kids, who have literally become *total strangers* living under the same roof; and most times - believe it or not - continue sharing the same bed! In their hearts, they feel downright bitterness and enmity for each other; each silently, but passionately, casting the blame for their self-inflicted misery, on the shoulders of the other. And the inevitable bitter divorce typically follows.

More often than not, though, some may even remain "together" in this *hellhole* until *Death Do Them Part* - literally! Please don't allow this picture to paint the story of your life – whoever you are.

As it stands, this is where we are; and for the most part, this is what continues to perpetuate in an alarming percentage of marriages in America today. Some jump from marriage to marriage, hoping to find happiness and mutual fulfillment. Nonetheless, most never-ever recognize that the *outside* pictures of what continues to manifest in their relationships and lives, are simply *external reflections* of what they're harboring on the *inside*, in their *own consciousness*.

I can indeed sit here, as many other writers have done, and itemize the many relationship issues in terms of what's referred to as naturally-occurring, gender-based, differences in viewpoint, followed by workable *forced* responses that would or should alleviate the prevailing conflicts, misunderstandings, and misinterpretations that have caused so many individuals to feel misplaced, mismatched, and correspondingly, stumped or powerless in their efforts to make marriages (relationships) work; however, I would not! In America today – and I am apt to think it has always been that way – we tend to believe that the solutions to our many life challenges *must always be complicated;* we simply don't believe in simplicity! It's somehow too easy to make sense to us.

Also, there is an ongoing tendency to not only approach problems believing the solutions must always be complicated, but to incessantly attempt to fix or treat resulting symptoms of the problems we face, instead of concentrating our efforts on finding-out and eliminating the true sources of our troubles. In my opinion, teaching an individual what to say and how to respond and not to respond to differences in viewpoints in relationships, from a gender perspective, can never be true solutions when deep inside they'll still be feeling that Ego-driven "need to be right" or "need to win" constantly nudging at them. If your value-system is *Ego-driven,* the *Ego* will always be victorious; therefore, true *harmony* in your relationships will inevitably be unsustainable.

As outlined throughout this chapter, I strongly believe when we finally come to terms with the fact that it is indeed our *Egos* that remain at the helm of every single problem we encounter or have ever encountered in our relationships and our entire lives – thus far, and further grasp that in order to live in harmony with nature and every other individual on the face of this earth, we must dismiss egotistical control of our *psyche* and allow *Self* to take full charge, only then would we gain the necessary insight we need to eliminate competing with each other on all levels; only then would we be able to experience true happiness in our lives; and only then, would we be able to dismiss our incessant "need to be always right" - among other things - in our relationships. Men will naturally start acting and being the way God intended them to be, and women would do likewise. If we can ever get to this place, we will literally be living like *Heaven on Earth!*

When we're able to achieve the preceding milestone "within" ourselves on a large enough scale, every single platform of egotistical control and influence "without" must naturally be altered: political; business operations and employment policies; governmental laws and policies; the Media – all Media; the Church, etc. It is now the year 2010, and I fervently believe that, as a society and world, we are presently making marked progress in this desirable direction. Presently, I am confident that what's clearly perceived as a *Recession,* in America, is actually a disguised *Renaissance* or "New Awakening" coming into being.

The good news is everything we desire, support, or give any level of credence to, *must* naturally change in support of us; but only after we change our *inner* perspective on things. All the pain and suffering we are presently experiencing in our marriages and otherwise, are simply a result of the *Ego-Driven System* we have blindly bought into, supported, and consequently allowed to fully control our level of life-value and awareness for an endless number of generations. The time to finally remove these blindfolds has come! The time for this urgent change is *NOW!*

# CHAPTER 6

# Commitment - As It Relates to Marriage

On the issue of *commitment* and it's direct relationship to *The Institution of Marriage*, way-back-when, a select group of professed Leaders, or other supposed authority figures, decided to perform an allegedly "gravely-needed," pagan-based, 'Wedding' of the terms "Marriage" and "Commitment" - all in desperate attempt to hopefully dismiss and further prevent the obvious prevailing flaws in the then failing, equally pagan-based, *Institution of Marriage*. Today, *The Institution* is still failing – miserably; this 'Wedding' proving to be more so an *added cause* of it's continued failure, rather than any remote *prevention* of it.

Sadly, we live under a system where just about everything is viewed from the perspective of, "If it does not work the way we expect it to, or if it malfunctions, fails or breaks (whatever 'it' may be), the only choices we have available to us is to either try and fix 'it,' seek to control or mask the resulting symptoms characteristic of its failure, or to simply eliminate 'it' altogether." With such modus operandi uppermost in our consciousness, we tend to approach virtually all of life's challenges - personal and otherwise - from this very same perspective: repeatedly making fervent yet futile effort to control or treat associated symptoms of our problems, rather than making it our business to isolate and unravel the true sources or root causes of the problems themselves! Our society had been so programmed to take this approach to all of life, and for so-so long, that the majority remains *blinded* to the possibility of any alternate course of action in challenging times.

Frankly, *The Institution* is failing, or has failed, largely because of what it is fundamentally – an "Institution!" Every such custom-driven convention is essentially based on some sort of pre-historic, outmoded, organized establishment using *Tradition* as its sole existing purpose and foundation. Typically, in the face of its failure, for example, we as a people are reared to seek refuge in the fear-driven religious aspect of *The Institution of Marriage* - all in desperate hope of remedying the tribulations we face. As a result, the failure continues - unchecked, while we keep asking ourselves the proverbial question, "Wonder why this breakdown continues to happen?"

The short answer is, most everyone thinks this and all other calamities would only be experienced by others. "That could never happen in my life or in my marriage!" This false sense of being "special," as compared to everyone else, is typically upheld until the particular adversity or mishap becomes their abiding reality. Then – in their minds – they have been personally ostracized by the entire World – and not excluding God!

As alluded to above, around the era when The Government and The Church was One, some professed Leaders came together and came up with what was referred to as "A Brilliant Idea," which went something like this: "Since men are the ones who often prove *unfaithful* in marriages, we will coerce him to swear in the presence of *God and Man* (as witnesses) to *commit* to his woman in *Holy Matrimony* (Marriage); setting it up in such a way that if he fails to honor his *commitment* - after the fact (this is where the Government comes in) - he will pay dearly, or lose material *things* of great value to himself." History has proven this to be nothing more than a "lame attempt" to solve yet another problem from the perspective of focusing on its associated symptoms.

For what it's worth, let's face it: Life is all about *Free Will!* And force *not to do* or *to do* something - anything - only increases ones desire and compulsion *to do* or *not to do* that very same thing. This is a fact of life as we know it. In other words, force accomplishes nothing!

My interpretation of the word, *commitment*, stems from the fact that *a commitment* has to do with personal accountability only - a personal decision, if you will. This implies that any repercussion for not keeping a *commitment* rests solely *on* and *with* that particular individual who made the said *commitment*. In other words, external repercussions *cannot* be justly applied here. If that person chooses to *punish* or *forgive* him or herself for breaking the said *commitment* - which can only be personal - it's his or her prerogative *alone* to do or not to do so. A *promise* is to another, and therefore, external; a *commitment* is a promise made to *oneself*, and therefore, can only be internal. They are not the same! You cannot justifiably make a *commitment* to someone else; you can only make a *commitment* to yourself!

Notice that "I" always comes before "commit" when used correctly. Often, we allow ourselves to become subjected to the external *senseless* version of using "you" before "commit," which, more often than not, imposes unprecedented pressures and unwarranted expectations on ourselves through others and vice versa. For example, according to the 2006 edition of The Collins Essential English Dictionary:

"A commitment is an obligation, responsibility or promise that restricts freedom of action."

Among other things, I believe Collins "Essential(ly)" forgot to include the word, "personal" in their definition. And please, please, please, try to make me understand why anyone would voluntarily involve themselves in *anything* that is referred to as "an obligation" or a restrictor of "freedom of action," while hoping to somehow obtain *happiness and bliss* out of it? I would really like to know exactly how this could ever possible be!

Also, notice carefully that under our System of Affairs making a *commitment* always has to do with giving-up something. For example:

"Sir, would you like to take advantage of this offer by *making a commitment* today towards your future prosperity? Go ahead and write a check for $5,000.00 (for example) to honor your *commitment!*"

This one is classical! And more often than not, what you're allegedly "getting" is almost always bogus! There seem to always be some external coercion to act, do, or spend something when the word or term is being used by others - especially when directed towards you. As a result, our typically skewed perception of the word *commitment*, traditionally, has to do with first making *a promise* – blindly, in most cases. Then to somehow prove you're serious about this *promise* you were coerced to make, you must put some *money* or something else of worldly value or importance to yourself, *on the line;* that which you're willing to forfeit, should you later change your mind or, more precisely, "break your *commitment!*"

This is what's typically deemed "The Commitment!" In other words, they require "a guarantee" out of you, by referring to the act as "a commitment" on your part; but you get no such assurance out of them. You can never truly know *the outcome* when you made this so-called *commitment*; therefore, this puts them (the ones forcing or coercing this "commitment," as they call it, out of you) in a very-likely win-win situation, whereas you'll be caught-up in a win or lose predicament! However, the proverbial question remains: *What exactly would you be really committing to?*

Let's redirect this viewpoint of *commitment,* and further apply it to what we loosely label as "Making a Commitment" in the arena of marriage. "Commitment" always seems to be the main focus or topic of conversation when unmarried women get together to discuss *Marriage;* and especially so, when men are at the center of such discussions. Also, for some reason, I can't recall ever hearing a man saying the words "She does not want to make a Commitment to me!" These words don't seem to ever find their way "into" and subsequently "out of" a man's mouth! Is it at all possible they could be gender-coded "For women only?" Finally, I think we may be on to something.

For most men, the word "Commitment" creates some rather unusual emotions. Women generally conclude that all *men* possess a typical "Fear of Commitment" - as they call it. However, after interviewing a considerable number of eligible *single* men - who are not, according to my findings, in any way opposed to marriage - followed by an equally significant number of married men, of the same age group (between 30 to 45 years old ), etc, I arrived at the following conclusions on the issue.

First and utmost, most men after being married for 5 or more years, still don't seem to really know or even understand what it was that they

"Committed to." One interviewee, Deon, who had been married for almost 13 years - with 2 kids - at the time, told me if he had the choice to make again, he would *never* get married. When I asked why? He responded as follows:

"I love the whole idea of raising my kids and doing family stuff.......but my wife and I really don't have a relationship anymore. We both uphold completely different views on life....I strive to stay in shape; she has gained over 100 lbs in the past 2 years. We have always been very active sexually; however, since the kids, she only seems to care to be intimate twice-a-month or so; and that's only when things are very good or she happens to be in *'heat'* at the time. This is very frustrating to me! I am always full of energy; she always seems to be extremely tired all the time - even though we share equally with the responsibilities of the kids. I always want to go-out and do things; she seldom wants to do anything, and rarely accompanies me anywhere. She eats terribly! And every time I dare to suggest eating better and exercise, it turns into a huge, ridiculous, argument. We're like total strangers! I really don't know how much more of this I can take!"

Deon's situation here represents the classic or general direction of the *pending cry*, or source of discontentment, which I have concluded to be the main *live-in destroyer of intimacy* for the majority of married men interviewed. By this I mean, they all gave me the impression that they genuinely felt as if their women changed completely "for the worse" in two (2) specific phases after marriage. *Phase one (1)* occurring immediately after the wedding – typically; and *Phase two (2)* commencing after the second child, or within 3 to 5 years of the particular marriage – whichever comes first. *Sounds like an Insurance Policy, doesn't it?* Let's examine some of the changes that *Phase one (1)* typically entails.

For most, *Phase one (1)* involved being subjected to major social reconstruction at the hands of their new wives. Suddenly, all their social activities are now being directed, monitored, and closely scrutinized. As a direct result of this, going-out with like-gender friends slowly becomes more and more intolerable, until it soon approaches and speedily reaches non-existence!

Further, if any of the husband's friends happens to be unmarried, rest-assured, it's a definite *no-no* for him to *hang-out* with such *men* from the *get-go!* In the typical woman's mind, "Single men are *always in search of* new women; therefore, if he's *hanging-out* with them.....he must be looking for new women also!" In other words, he does not know what he wants – he's *fickle*; he's unable to think and make sensible decisions for himself; therefore, she (his wife) *must now* make it her business to do the *thinking* and *decision-making* for him. She knows what's best for him! Could this be solely to "protect" herself?

Also, in *Phase one (1)*, the Couple *must* now do and start practicing the "Marriage Thing!" What exactly is the "Marriage Thing?" This refers to the perceived notion that outside of *work* or the couple's individual career obligations to the family unit, it is now absolutely necessary for them to be inseparable, to *do absolutely everything together* as much as humanly possible. After all, as per the prevailing *Institution's* directive, they are now "A Couple" (One), and that's what married couples are "supposed to do." In other words, there's no more "what we as a couple *uniquely* enjoyed doing prior to marriage;" that's thrown-out and into the dumpster - forever! It, instead, becomes a situation where the couple now "joins the line" with everyone else by doing and adhering to what "they say" makes marriage sense. Have you ever wondered why couples, who were together for many *happy years* prior to marriage, suddenly fall apart after the fact? Think real hard about this reality! What you've always thought to be the reason for this may not be accurate.

In addition, there's a traditionally-dictated, transformational, behind-the-scenes, required "name change" that immediately takes effect between newly-weds from the onset of the marriage ceremony. What I find to be rather amusing, though, is this "name change" is always identical across the *Institutional* board. Suddenly, the man's name changes, in reference, to "My Husband;" and correspondingly, the woman's name suddenly changes, in reference also, to "My Wife" or "My Beautiful Wife" - if she happens to be present.

This "name change" is absolutely necessary – especially so for husbands when referencing their wives. So much so, that if not adhered to, they more often than not would be faced with endless unforeseen DRAMA from their wives; all filled with accusations of not being happy, of not feeling complete, and of not being satisfied, honest, and proud of their decision or commitment to marry them. It gets that deep!

When it's all said and done, the *Man* is perceived as the gender who *voluntarily* decided – whether by open coercion, threat of abandonment, instilled fear of loss of Love, or otherwise – to relinquish his naturally-occurring, corrupted, often womanizing ways by making a *commitment* (which is directly interchangeable with solely his 'decision' to ask for the woman's hand in marriage, under our practicing *Institution of Marriage*) to this woman; the alleged Savior of him from his vile, contaminated ways. In light of this, he must also be willing to "stick-with" and "live-by" the expected protocol surrounding his decision, according to the directives of the *Institution*. This is the point where the common, unhealthy "Ownership Factor" typically gains its initial approval to exist.

If the particular marriage lasts for more than approximately 3 years, *Phase two (2)* typically kicks-in. Again, the changes occurring in this phase frequently start during the 2nd pregnancy or after the 2nd child arrives. The characteristics of this 2nd *Phase* are typically as follows:

Suddenly, sex with their wives becomes a "scarce commodity!" The *kids* always seem to "come first" – even when they're "dead-asleep!" Also, their wives are almost *always too tired* to engage in the act of sex – except on very rear occasions; maybe once or twice a month when they're in 'heat.' The staple complaint or excuse always seems to hover around *not feeling appreciated by the husband*, or being overly stressed-out and exhausted for an endless array of reasons.

In addition to all this, to my surprise and amazement, I soon learned that there is a *known* and reluctantly-accepted *reality* among married men: "Married Men Don't Get Sex (from their wives)!" This had me completely astounded! Nonetheless, the concern came across as being one of the most bothersome grievances among all the married men interviewed. My immediate response was: "So why *the hell* would you men stay married?" The answers I got were mind-boggling! They included:

"It's *always* cheaper to keep her!"

"If I leave, I will be *Cleaned-Out!*.........Remember, I *do have* 2 kids!.......The Government will have a *Field Day* with my paycheck!"

"To keep myself sane.......I do visit *Strip Clubs* (Gentlemen Clubs) whenever and wherever I get a chance.......It works for me!"

"Sex is not *EVERYTHING!*"

"I secretly have and maintain a *Little Thing* (a woman or mistress) on the side........That keeps me contented!"

Also, *Phase two (2)* may sometimes involve a fervent attempt to change the husband's wardrobe to somehow match the "New Image" his wife now has of or for him. It's as if she wants to say, "I've got to make sure none of the *Vultures* (women) out there take him away from me; therefore, I must start *dressing* him – *my way*...to keep him looking *dull and uninteresting;* and at-the-same-time, send a message which clearly says he's married and *off-limits!*"

The paradox here is, the typical woman would zealously want to keep her husband grounded in what she wants, solely for the vanity of preventing the possibility of having herself viewed as *a failure* – external to the marriage(i.e. to her friends, peers, family members, etc); however, *within* the confines of the particular marriage - the so-called *commitment* itself - her actions or lack of it thereof, may be actively and unknowingly pushing him into the very arms of the same women she's passionately attempting to *protect* him, or her own interest, from.

This need to, what I call, falsely protect "her own interest," often spills-over into the particular man's health and well-being during this 2nd phase. A few of the men interviewed - the ones who seem to be very much into preserving their own personal health and well-being through exercise, dieting, etc - commented on how frequently their wives would make what they referred to as "ridiculous observations" concerning this continued interest within them. These include statements such as, "Why are you *still* exercising?....Married men are supposed to put on weight and have *growing* bellies; it shows they're happy, settled, and well taken cared of!" Or the infamous, "You're married now....why do you think you need to stay in shape anymore....are you looking for someone else?" In other words, this *commitment* he made is supposed to serve as a "Death Sentence" to his health and wellbeing! Amazing!

The Bible clearly speaks-out on and strongly recommends that individuals seeking marriage *should* be "equally yoked." However, once again, the meaning of this term has been misinterpreted - mainly by the Church - to only apply to individuals who "say" they believe in God and Jesus Christ. In fact, in the Bible, when the term was originally documented (before it was misconstrued by later interpreters – whether deliberate or otherwise), it was solely referring to certain species of animals that should or should not be yoked or bred together to produce offspring.

Often, individuals are taught to believe that solely because they allegedly grew-up in what we refer to as a "Christian Home," and attend church every Sunday; and so, correspondingly call themselves "Christians," this makes them "equally yoked." They would typically view this seeming *fact,* alone, as the ultimate deciding reason among reasons for getting married. Accordingly, it is the one thing that would *make or break* the validity of a pending union of marriage, especially in the area of being ultimately pleasing or displeasing to God - in their eyes!

As an acquaintance of mine once put it:

"...There's much more politics in *The Church* than in the White House!"

Let it be known that believing in God and Jesus Christ - just believing in their existence - has *nothing* to do with *Spirituality!* However, emulating God, through practicing the teachings of any of the known Prophets or Spiritual Teachers, does! They can never be the same! The true essence of these teachings, centers around one major oversight of mankind: *Spirituality!* Instead of gaining insight into the spiritual lessons and practices taught and exemplified by these Sages, as a society and world, we collectively allow our *Egos* to lead us down the path to blistering self-confusion; and mainly as a direct consequence of the "Ones" we have chosen to refer to as our Earthly Spiritual Teachers - forever on the beaten path to their *Man-Made Salvation* under the direction of the greatest source of division *unknown to Man*: Religion! If they themselves are confused, where exactly does that leave you and me?

The insightful approach to being "Equally yoked," as applied to relationships and marriages, sensibly refers to the necessity for both individuals to possess deep-rooted fundamentals that are in-sync with each other on all levels. However, not even this practical approach is remotely adhered to in our society, since the ""Christian home," and attend church every Sunday.." belief system is revered as being divinely and traditionally "right," even though, in my opinion, it does not and has not *truly* worked - ever!

If spirituality was indeed practiced and encouraged in The Church, fostering individuals into entering the true spiritual realm within themselves, which would lead to them unquestionably emulating the very essence and likeness of God – as intended, then it just might be possible to apply the term "equally yoked" to a relationship that comes out of such divinity. However, today, it is hardly likely to find much of this anywhere. As a people, we have mostly overlooked our own spirituality, our own divinity for, as Dr. Wayne Dyer puts it: "**Earth-Guided-Only**" (**ego**tistical) control.

As is obvious in Deon's case above, time always reveals the truth about compatibility; the truth about the abiding love individuals claim to possess for each another; and ultimately, the truth about being *equally or unequally yoked*. In our society today, many of us unknowingly look at this *Love and Commitment* thing under the *blindfolds* of what I deem to be "Blissful Convenience." Why? We typically see it as "The *right* thing to do at a particular age (over 30 - usually)." "Let's just do it and hope for the best...... It *is* what everyone else is doing – right?" And generally, this is the approach most of us uphold in just about every aspect of our lives: "From the cradle to the grave....our civil *duty* is to follow the crowd!" However, the self-imposed *blindness* goes much deeper than this.

As it stands, one person may choose to inform another of a *commitment* they have made with respect to that *other person*, the proof of which lies *only* in personal trust or faith - alone. Yet, our pagan-based *Institution of Marriage,* along with its necessary forerunners, deems it necessary to suggest *forcing* its version of *commitment* - especially *so* unto men, in a fashion that can almost be mistaken for being passive, but is absolutely not! Have you ever wondered why some men literally "freeze-up" when the word "commitment" is being used by their women? It's not because they don't want to "commit" in the true sense of the word. It's simply because - once again - they don't really know what it is they would be committing to! Remember, men have proven to be the more logical gender.

First, let's consider the fact that approximately ninety percent (90%) of the married men interviewed for this project, kept-on "singing the same song:" After-the-fact, they felt as if "getting married" was really only to bring the Government into their homes on the side of, and in *full* support of, their women *only!* We see evidence of this in our society just about every day. For example, would any man be taken seriously if he were to call *the authorities* to his home, and claim to have been physically abused or raped by his *own* wife? I don't think so! However, on-the-flip-side, if this same call were to be made by his wife, he would literally be put in jail "in a heartbeat" - irrespective of any indication of the obvious truth of what really "went down." This is the common *Truth* that is all too evident in the society we live in. Men have simply become a direct by-product of this *Truth!*

Secondly, as mentioned earlier, after being "shafted" so many times under the heading of "making a commitment" - a common fad in our society - unmarried men seem to strongly anticipate *a loss* of some kind, which appears to represent the inescapable outcome of making any kind of commitment. Some may even react to the term in a way that symbolizes reluctance towards give-in to an impending death sentence! Why? Accordingly, as communicated by the majority of unmarried men, this viewpoint can be partially attributed to the observation of their married counterparts, whose obvious disposition and well-being always seem to significantly deteriorate in short duration after making "the commitment" as we call it.

To this end, both the married and unmarried men voiced a main concern of not really wanting anything *forced upon them!* Some were of the opinion that the word "commitment" alone, relating to marriage, sounds and feels forced - although most would never openly share this viewpoint with their women or wives.

Conclusively, I believe more men would want to go through with the act of "getting married" only after the coercive, unrecognized, fear-based forces surrounding "commitment" are altogether flushed-out and eliminated. Men are not robots! And they're definitely not "cold," as far too many women seem to believe. Men are simply *Logical Beings!* Smart women, do what it takes to understand what this means; and usually, this type turns-out to be the ones who are happy and unusually happily married. Women, who know this, simply become "The Logical Choice" for the men they choose to share their lives with. And it's all *gravy* after that. No trying to *force his hand,* after concluding he "now loves her," by giving him "Marriage Ultimatums" to either *do* or *die.* Or suddenly joining the local church and claiming to be *now* "saved" and therefore, cannot be intimate with him any longer - outside of marriage. Or *now* requiring an "equally-yoked" partner; one who's willing to do the honorable thing (*commit to her*) in order to please God. Etc.

I've discovered that most women subconsciously think they *must have* this *commitment* from the men in their lives for a number of reasons; most of which are the direct consequence of childhood-conditioning and adapted cultural codes, propelled entirely by inherited traditional practices. The following are two examples of this:

## The Guarantee

Firstly, some seek this *commitment,* since, in their minds - as subliminal as it may be - they believe they deserve to be provided with "a guarantee" or some other form of "security measure," so they can possibly "laugh all-the-way to the bank" if the man "messes-up" or gets caught in the act of *cheating* (which, in western societies, seems to be the number one unwritten necessity for this "commitment"). This, in itself, is the root underlying reason why men with "lots of money," instantly become the ones most desirable for marriage, as opposed to those without "lots of money" - irrespective of any other negative or positive trait they may possess.

This common practice, remains effectual on the basis of what I refer to as "The Security Shelter" for if and when he "messes-up; since he's *A Man,* and it's always expected of him!" In other words, the man is expected to "mess-up;" therefore, this needed "commitment" and other security measures, are somewhat of a financial and mental *guarantee* - if you will - of a "pay-back," for what the woman thinks she'll be "giving-up" when she accepts the proposal of marriage from the man. So, paradoxically, the "guarantee" he affords her, also serves as his deterrent from "messing-up."

Strangely enough, in the average woman's mind, the man has "nothing to lose" if she "messes-up" – as they call it – since she is "The Prize" to be had, and being with her – even once – is all the "pay-back," security, or guarantee he could ever ask for. This is the typical *double standard* in passive practice today throughout most, if not all, western societies.

## The Proposal

Secondly, notice that in the name of *Tradition,* the man is *required* to drop to one knee in a position of plea, praise, and worship to humbly ask for the woman's hand in marriage. In addition, to further prove his "readiness to commit," the engagement ring he buys and brings to this momentous occasion *must* be worth 2 to 3 times his monthly salary in order to qualify. In the woman's mind, this entire act clearly symbolizes what is referred to as "his solemn promise to commit." To this end, the typical woman in most western societies would *NOT* accept this proposal as valid, unless the entire act or ritual has transpired – verbatim – as *Tradition* (and Mommy usually) dictates.

## The Role Men Play In All This

The above phenomenon continues to perpetuate – unchecked – in our society; and largely because, most men have passively bought-into fervently supporting this type mind-set. Why? Because many are actually living their lives expecting to find a woman who would, in some way or another, "guarantee their happiness" - simply by virtue of being a woman! So what they do is accept "whatever," while hoping to experience *Eternal Bliss* from it through doing and becoming *"whatever"* the particular woman expect of them, instead of remaining true to who they are *on the inside* - where it really counts.

The above suggestion may seem completely insignificant to some; but, nonetheless, it can and does have profound, far-reaching, negative repercussions on both sides. Some men would say, "She says she wants a *commitment*......so I'll give her what she wants – just to keep her *happy*!" While, at the same time, eagerly hoping that this act alone would in-turn ensure the needed *happiness* he thinks he *should* experience as a result of it. The question is: Is this *what* he truly feels and wants also?

Notice that the average woman seems to always think "Security" would somehow bring her "Happiness;" whereas the average man, on the other hand, seems to always think his "Happiness" is solely dependent on the woman's acceptance of him through the required protocol of commitment and security he provides and adheres to. Ironically, the problem is, they have been traveling *down* different roads, which both lead to the same predictable, but unforeseen, *dead end*! This arrangement may seem to work for a while, but ultimately, *failure* becomes certain! This "blind act," as I like to call it, is probably the #1 forerunner of most failed or failing marriages in our society today.

You are probably thinking to yourself, "What the *'hell'* is this guy talking about...Is there any other way to view this?" And to this, I'll respond, *"There is* indeed!" A wise, God-realized man named Lao-Tzu, is said to have observed some 2500+ years ago as he dictated the verses of his World renowned *Tao Te Ching* that,

".....Things that are *forced* may grow for a while, but then soon *wither away*........"

Among other things, this brings to mind the commonly used saying: "The End Justifies the Means." This suggests that since *the final outcome* is really what matters in the "End," then whatever transpired leading to this "End," clearly constitutes "the Means."

Many of us may perceive any of this as being "forced" in any way, primarily because of what we have grown to accept as being *normal,* and due to the fact that it's all we, our parents, our grandparents, and even our great grandparents and beyond regard and accept as being *truth-to-life.* We really only passively accept all such things to be "our reality," as a direct result of what has been passed down to us through these unbroken, yet self- corrupting hereditary channels.

As mentioned previously in this chapter, and throughout this Book, I cannot emphasize enough how much, to our detriment, our lives have been thwarted and bombarded by an unending plethora of traditional belief-patterns, which continue to instill and perpetuate insurmountable amounts of fear-based thoughts into our minds. These thoughts unavoidably crystallizing into the daily life-patterns and circumstances we erroneously refer to as our *abiding reality.* The truth is, no act of compliance by one person can in any way, shape, or form make or keep any other person "Happy," by any means! As Dr. Wayne W. Dyer once wrote:

"There's *no way* to happiness; happiness is (indeed) *the way!*"

This simply means that "the *only* way" to this *sustained happiness* we crave, is *already* inherent in every individual. In reality, this state of being cannot be acquired or truly experienced through, by, or from any other person or material thing - *outside* of that particular individual. If we continue to expect *temporary* (external) *pleasure* to bring us *sustained* (internal) *happiness,* we have actually bought-into a life of never-ending disappointments, mental chaos, and unending inner and outer turmoil! Does the astronomical divorce rate in America ring any bells? I guess some would say "There are no guarantees in life!" If we truly understand and accept the fact that there are indeed no guarantees in life, then why are we *constantly expecting guarantees* from or through others?" Think about that!

# CHAPTER 7

## What Should a REAL Woman Want and Expect of Her Man?

One beautiful summer afternoon in New York City, some years ago, while driving in the front passenger side of her red Renault Le Car, a then girlfriend blatantly cut-off a fully-loaded tractor trailer, all in a frantic rush to get onto the north entrance ramp of the Bronx River Parkway. Shook-up from the close call (especially so, since it would have been my side of the vehicle that would have sustained the initial impact of the possible *deadly crash*), I ventured to ask the reason for her senselessly-reckless maneuver. In a calm, un-moved, single breath she passively replied:

"I know he saw it was a woman......I have *the right* to go first!"

Astounded by her candid response, it was immediately apparent to me that this girl was completely *willing* to jeopardize her life - and mine - all on the premise of an "expectation" or "right-to-expect" of a man – any man – what she inherently thinks she "deserves" as a woman! Uncanny!

While in school, at about age16, I dated a girl in my 10th grade class, who one day *demanded of me* to buy her *something* (I can't seem to quite recall exactly what it was). When I replied that I was unable to do so (this was due to the fact that I didn't have a job and extra money at the time; the very same situation she was in), she looked at me from 'head to toe' several times, and with an obvious disgusted, contemptuous, facial gesture blurted-out,

"How *the hell* do you expect to have a girlfriend if you don't have money?"

And she avoided having anything else to do with me after that incident.

More recently, one night on South Beach, Miami, while on a first date, the young woman made a rather peculiar remark to me concerning the fact that she found it to be "unmanly" that I would walk on the *inside* section of the sidewalk, while I *allowed* her to walk on the *outside* or traffic side . When I inquired as to the significance of her remark, she further explained that it was what she "expects of a man," based on her up-bringing. I guess the traditionally-inspired *expectation* is for the man to be on the side towards the roadway to somehow "protect" the woman from water-puddle splashes, perpetrators, automobile accidents, and all other danger-related possibilities. I mean, I am always open, ready, and willing to protect the woman I am with - if need be, but to address such a superficial issue on a first date, under the premise of an ingrained *expectation*, in my mind, was equivalent to her walking out into the middle of the street, with loud-speaker in hand, and suddenly screaming-out at the top of her lung: "Lookout: *Drama Queen* coming through!"

I do have many more related situations to share; both from my own experiences and from those other men have shared with me. However, to include them all here would be beyond the scope of this book. I used the ones above, just to give you a preliminary snapshot of the widespread array of "wants" and "expectations" some women seem to passively pass unto men as their seeming *justifiable right*! They seem to have a different list for all the levels of men they could possibly encounter in their lives: from innocent by-standers, to sharing the roads; from mere acquaintances, to close friendships; from brothers and brother-in-laws, to father and father-in-laws; and finally, from boyfriends, to 'man,' to husbands. The husband's list being the one which typically has no conceivable end!

I will get to the men in the next chapter, but here, I want to make one thing resoundingly clear to *each* and *every* woman: *A woman should want and expect absolutely NOTHING of her man!* She should instead, turn *all* of her *wants* and *expectations* unto herself, and simply allow *her Man* to just be who he is. If who he is – *as he is* – does not resonate well with her – *as she is* - even though she turned all her *wants* and *expectations* unto herself, then they should both consider going their separate ways; allowing things to be what they're going to be - anyway! This outlook is possibly the only *workable* path to happiness and true contentment in personal relationships. Here's why?

I know you've probably never heard of or read anything as bewildering in your entire life! I'll take a wild guess here and conclude that this would probably be so, simply because you were *conditioned* to see life as being perfectly *normal* to place unending *wants* and *expectations* onto others – especially the other individual in your Love relationships, and obviously through not realizing the lifelong internal and external confusion, mayhem, and related and unrelated turmoil such an outlook can and will create in your life – if not there already!

"We all have expectations" some would emphatically declare! And I do understand that on a job, for example, an employee is *expected to perform* his or her duties in order to "get-paid" and, of course, keep his or her job (the reason for the infamous *Supervisor*). But consider for a moment, if one were to place this *expectation to perform* onto oneself. Clearly, the worry and stress of performance related job loss would then be greatly decreased and perhaps eliminated altogether. As a result, we'd have a happier, more productive, stress-free employee. Think about that!

Nonetheless, even though I can see definite comparative value in the above scenario, and all of life *does* involve relationships – as I like to say, here I am specifically concerned with the "wants" and "expectations" of women when it comes to their men. This is quite a different *animal* altogether! I once met a woman who told me she divorced her husband because he still wanted to go hang-out with his unmarried friends after they were married. I know a very wealthy ex-professional athlete, whose wife divorced him due to the fact that he decided to leave the profession to become a Fisherman; a passion he always wanted to pursue. It was communicated to me that after the divorce was final, she said words to the effect of, "I married a professional athlete...and *I expected* it to stay that way....It didn't!" I know yet another woman who, after three years of dating, followed by another three years of marriage, filed for divorce on the grounds that she *suddenly* came to the realization that the man she had been with for six, long, years was not her "Intellectual Equal!"

I can continue-on here forever with these stories of shipwrecked lives resulting from women's seeming justifiable, incessant "wants" and "expectations" of the men they call husbands, but I think I've clearly made my point. I will also add here that even though it may not be readily recognizable, these demands are more often than not, specifically, women's Ego demands – placed on the ones who supposedly *Love* them; the ones who *must* continue to prove their Love; the ones who have made the expected "commitment," yet it's still *never* enough; etc.

Understand, once again: when you allow the *Ego* to direct your life, you're always in for a very stormy ride. No matter how hard you may try, this *Ego* of yours can never-ever be satisfied! Consequently, allowing egotistical control of your psyche, will *always* lead to you being forever disappointed in your relationships and in all other areas of your life, for that matter. *Disappointment* often leads to frustration; *Frustration* leads to discontentment; *Discontentment* leads to Irritability; *Irritability* leads to *Resentment*; and *I know* you're all too familiar with exactly where this ultimately leads. Then, what are we left with? We're typically left with a gender who finds it absolutely necessary to blame *The World* for its self-imposed predicament, as is evident in such familiar comments as, "There are no *Good Men* left out there!" And the all too common, "All the *Good Men* are already taken!"

I say "....*NOTHING* of her Man," because when a woman is able to, instead, turn all her *"wants"* and *"expectations"* unto herself, this channels her energies into the state of being that I call "ALLOWING;" this possibly being the only effective path to a truly blissful existence in relationships (and in all of life as we know it). Basically, *ALLOWING* is the state of being where *One* is – as Dr. Wayne Dyer puts it – "able to dismiss (their) Ego's Agenda.." to fulfill its endless list of *wants* and *expectations* of others. How can this *ALLOWING* be effectively accomplished in relationships?

The key here is to *ALLOW* him to simply *be* himself, without any pressures from you to be otherwise; and to further, "see yourself" in him. This means, to identify with the *true essence of your own existence* (your *Spiritual Self*), which also exists as an integral part of him (his *Spiritual Self*) - as he is; and to just *let it be* what it's going to be anyway! I know this sounds somewhat unorthodox to most, but, the truth remains, when we are able to identify with that "true essence" of ourselves in others - as they are, and accept it as the way it "should be," rather than try to force it to be *something else*, we'll quickly and naturally dismiss our need and fervent desire to change others into what we *selfishly expect* them to be *to* and *for* us - based on the lifelong, hereditary conditioning we have unconsciously bought-into and accepted as our inescapable reality.

The primary benefit here is when we are able to adapt the preceding approach into our lives and relationships, the positive *energy* we'll naturally radiate, will likewise encourage others to also emit similar *energy-patterns* towards us. This result in a powerful, mutually-gratifying, indescribable attractive force between individuals; all grounded in a deep-rooted self-respect and total appreciation for oneself.

Have you ever noticed how wonderfully blissful you feel in the beginning stages of a relationship? It's like *"Wow!* I feel so ecstatically-wonderful with and around this person....I truly believe it has got to be *God* somehow - somewhere - orchestrating all this, *solely* in my favor!" Everything goes so *right*! He or she intuitively says and does the "right things" all the time. You talk on the phone for hours at a time - mostly about *nothing,* but somehow, you find yourselves enjoying every moment of it, non-the-less. You may even ask questions of each other, such as, "Where have you been all my life?" "Do you believe this could be *Destiny?*" And in some cases, "Do you believe in *Love at first sight?*" Etc. Time together seems to *speed-on-by;* and all your waking thoughts center only on him or her. For most, life is just breathtakingly-joyous at these times.

However, after a short while - some a few months; others longer - everything typically changes; you soon start feeling differently about him or her. What is typically responsible for this common change? The process is rather simple! We can equate it to the birth of a child, for example. In the beginning stage, a child is born and not being yet conditioned to *the ways of the world* (no judgments or expectations of others), its every action and emotion is unknowingly filled with absolute awe: "Oh wow! I am learning to touch my toes!" "I am touching Mommy's nose!" "Daddy sounds funny!" Etc. We can actually observe this child and, if discern enough, we'd be able to see divine approbation at work in everything he or she does. The kid is truly in the state of a peaceful, heavenly, existence at this time – although most of us, as adults, may not recognize this.

Ok, so you just got into a new relationship; you just started "kicking-it" with this new person you really-really feel completely *connected* to. Everything is going nicely. You both feel wonderfully great! It's all eternally perfect - in your minds. Guess what's directly responsible for these amazingly exquisite feelings you're both engrossed-in at this blissful time? It's because – *simply because* – you're both operating in a state of ALLOWING! Just like the baby - being new to the world and life - approaches it all with no judgments or expectations, but with awesome appreciation in the hue of understanding how his or her own existence fits into the cyclical nature of things and life itself, you are simply ALLOWING that other person to *just be* who they are! You are ALLOWING them to just exist! More precisely, you are actively "seeing" and understanding "yourself" (learning and discovering new and more appreciative things *about yourself*) in and through them – naturally! It is simply nature at work; and at such times, you are unconsciously working in harmony with nature– whether you know it or not.

This is the sole reason why in the beginning stages of a relationship, you feel so-so wonderfully-blissful with and about that other person. Now you know! What you experience then, is the truth about *who* you really are; therefore, it's a clear indication of how you're actually able to live when you tap into your true *internal* bliss! I am sure you have been there many times before.

Remember this: Whatever you feel ONLY comes from you. This means that *all the Love* you can possibly have and feel, already exists within you. It is not because he put his "best foot forward" in the beginning, and that's the reason why you were feeling "so good" at first. And incidentally, if that's what he was doing, then you were indeed doing the very same thing, also. I've heard too many women say some version of,

"When I met him he pretended to be *one person*, and later-on he changed into really being *someone else*!" The question is: Did he really pretend to be what he's not; did he really change? No, not necessarily so! You simply met each other, and you both were in a state of ALLOWING (and believe me, I am not saying they're any Saints on the side of the males; I am just looking at the female perspective at this point). At that time, you were feeling GREAT! Then, in short duration, you started CONTAMINATING your state of ALLOWING; you started introducing "wants" and "expectations" into the equation. "Wants" and "expectations," based on what *you believe* or how *you think* he should be and act towards you. So, in other words, you stopped ALLOWING, and you began DEMANDING things of him. This new DEMANDING attitude, then leads to you becoming disappointed, since all your Ego's demands can never be met at all times; and soon, you start going-through the whole gamut of emotions, as a result of voluntarily replacing your own state of ALLOWING with a new state of continual disappointment (discussed earlier). All this, ultimately leading to pandemonium in the given relationship; and soon, it typically ends bitterly!

Often, this is how things usually transpire; but for some reason, many don't seem to ever grasp what it is that they keep doing to instigate such an outcome. If we venture to apply this ALLOWING principle to our everyday lives; if we can somehow learn to appreciate that every hour in our lives is filled with 60 minutes, which is in itself filled with 60 seconds of NOW time, we would effortlessly *stop* clinging to circumstances and outcomes, and we'd correspondingly *stop* expecting or forcing others to be *how* or *what* we want or expect them to be. In other words, we'll start living this blissful state of ALLOWING every single moment of our lives.

The renowned Lebanese poet, Kahlil Gibran, puts it perfectly in his piece *My Soul Preached To Me*. He wrote,

"…..I imagined the Past as an epoch that never returned, and the Future as one that could never be reached.

Now I realize that *the present moment* contains *all time* and within it is all that can be *hoped for*, *done* and *realized*..."

Believe this!

I know the opinion of some may be something to the effect of,

"This guy is talking crazy, Utopia stuff! *It is normal* to worry about the future; therefore, living in the *NOW*, would be living irresponsibly!" But you can't *know*, until you *know*! When you're able to 'get there' you'll understand. It's down-right phenomenal! In my own life, I've been practicing this way of being for approximately three year or so. I went from a state of going back and forth, for a while, to now practicing it fulltime. It's the best I've ever felt about my life! I presently live only in *NOW* moments; I do *everything* in the *NOW*. As a result, I no longer cling to circumstances or expectations – especially of others, and I *ALLOW* myself - and others - to just *be* themselves.

Remember always, this *ALLOWING* starts with you. It affords you the ability to put all your focus into this very present "NOW" moment. In this way, you'll *amazingly* stop clinging to the past, since it can never be in the *NOW*, and *surprisingly*, you'll stop worrying about the future from the usual fear-based perspective of the incessant "what ifs.." which plagues most of our lives. You'll *NOW* start enjoying every moment of your life, since that's really all that you have. And in short duration - no matter what befalls you - the mere thought of being *stressed-out* about *ANYTHING* will seem entirely ludicrous to you. In other words, you'd be able to feel and experience only positive possibilities for yourself, in the *NOW*, which in essence will be orchestrating all your possibilities for the future and beyond! It's truly amazing!

I discussed my definition of *Love* in an earlier chapter. To recap, my definition of *Love* is: *The Unselfish Respect and Appreciation One Holds for*

*One's Own Existence* (*Love* for self); and *therefore*, for the *Existence* of another (*Love* for *all* others). The latter being *non-existent*, unless *the former* already exists. In other words, you cannot *honestly* feel *Love* for anyone else, until you first *honestly* feel complete *Love* for yourself!

On the grounds of this being accepted as *truth*, I consider my definition of *Love* to be directly interchangeable with *ALLOWING* (described above). You've got to understand that you can only *Love* a person as much as they *ALLOW* you to feel *Love* for them! Are you getting this? When I mention, "*ALLOW* you to feel *Love* for them," I mean, how much they are *ALLOWING* you to simply *be yourself* is directly related to the level of *Love* you can "have" and "hold" for that person – and vice-versa. This means that how much they are *ALLOWING* you and/or how much you are *ALLOWING* them, is really what we relate to as profound, unshakeable, *able to stand the test of time*, *Love* when and where it exists. Think about the following: God (*Universal Intelligence / The Source* - being the epitome of *Love* itself) can only *Love* you as much as you are *ALLOWING* God to *Love* you; and even-though, God does have an insurmountable amount of *Love* for you, you cannot feel, know, or even realize this *Love* until you *ALLOW* yourself to become spiritually conscious of its existence and depth. In my opinion, reading the Bible alone can never accomplish this. Take this understanding – if you *got it* – and apply it to your personal relationship(s).

Nevertheless, in our society, even-though this *ALLOWING* is absolutely necessary to a harmonious existence in relationships, most tend to cling to a warped understanding of what *Love* really is or, more accurately, *should be!* We believe and act upon *Love* to mean (especially so on the side of women, in my experience) that "You've got to do and be *what I want* you to do and be, and this is what *I know Love* to be.....because this means *I Love You* or *You Love Me!*" In other words, in their minds, *Love* is exclusively dependent on what one person does to *please* the other, rather than being appreciated for who they really are.

However, in reality, how you feel: the *desire*, the *need*, the *want*, the *craving* to spend time with and to share life with another, hopefully from a *non-fear-driven* perspective, is altogether a direct reflection of how much that other person is *ALLOWING* you to *simply* be yourself, to *Love* them in your *own* unique way through being allowed to feel complete respect and appreciation for your own existence – Loving yourself. No other outlook can sustain a fulfilling relationship!

Say, for example, there's an issue where you see some kind of self-destructive element or habit in him (or her). Understand that you cannot *encourage* him based on what you want for *yourself*, because then, that would be an "expectation" on your part. If you see him going down the *wrong path*, abusing drugs or alcohol, for example, and you honestly want to encourage him to do better, then this is where *ALLOWING* comes into play: Here, you'd first and utmost, continue to *ALLOW* him to be himself; but in addition, you'd also want to be introducing *encouragement*, since you'd now be actually implementing the process of understanding or "seeing yourself in him (described earlier)." With this approach, the common practice of *blame* is removed from the situation; and with this common blame factor eliminated, you'd now be in a better position to motivate him to understand that life is more, and life is all about preserving life, rather than destroying it. Adapting this perspective of *ALLOWING* is probably one of the most effective ways of helping a Love-partner when in any kind of self-inflicted distress, such as an addiction, etc.

To reiterate: My whole point here is to examine *Love*, in itself, as being *The Unselfish Respect and Appreciation One Holds For One's Own Existence*; and if this is *true* for yourself, then it's automatic that you'll *Hold* or *feel* the same toward all others as well. Also, this feeling or practice of *ALLOWING* you have (hopefully) gravitated-to in your own life, is what you'll unconsciously have to offer, hand-off or radiate to others. You can only *give* what you already *have* within yourself! In other words, while you're in this state of *ALLOWING*, you'd be *ALLOWING* whomever to be who they are; and by how much you are *ALLOWING* them, that's how much they are able to what we call, "Love you." By the same token, by how much they are *ALLOWING* you, will reflect how much you are able to, what we call,

"Love them." Therefore, in reality, *Love* and ALLOWING seem to go hand in hand. This is basically ALLOWING in a nutshell. Let's look at a typical example of the effectiveness of this concept.

Woman or wife gets into a relationship or marriage; she *loves* flowers, for example. According to her, her conceptual understanding is "I Love flowers." But far too many women don't see it as simply "I Love flowers;" they, instead, see it as "I Love to *receive* flowers!" So she happens to be with this guy or husband and, as I alluded to above, to her, it's an integral part of *Love* that "He should give me flowers to *show* his *Love!*" Or "He *should do* what *I expect* of him if he truly *Loves* me!" However, it so happens that this particular guy wasn't raised that way; he does not really see value in giving roses and flowers and all such things. It's not that he doesn't *Love* her; it's just the way he views life as a result of his up-bringing.

Ok, you are the typical woman - you Love flowers, and you somehow find yourself in the foregoing predicament. Here's what I mean by putting your "wants" and "expectations" unto yourself. Again, you *Love* everything about roses, flowers, etc; therefore, guess what you do? *Expectations unto yourself:* get yourself flowers! I know at this point some women may be thinking some version of the following:

"What the Hell? Why should I be buying myself flowers......I do have a Man?"

Whatever! Understand again: Hopefully, you want to *have a life*, you intend to be happy, and you also want to be in a blissful relationship! Am I accurate in my assumptions here; I could be wrong? It's all up to you! You can "force him" to do what you want him to do, and consequently, make him miserable - and think that it's all ok; or you can try to live in a harmonious way, by just simply ALLOWING him to be himself!

Ok, again: You *Love* flowers - get your own flowers! You buy your own *lovely flowers*; and I am confident that, sooner or later, he's bound to say – if he's picking-up on your positive, ALLOWING energy ( that is: *only* if it's not a false pretense, on your part, filled with impatience, anxiety, and inner resentment towards him) – something to the effect of:

"Honey...I like those!" Or "Those are very nice!"

And guess what? If you want to go further (And remember, the key here is you *must not* be *expecting* anything of him - especially in terms of these flowers; you don't expect, because "expectations," again, lead to disappointments, and you know – all too well – where this leads), you could sometime get him some roses that you think he may appreciate. Remember, you've been observing his reaction to your roses. When you do, he would probably be startled. He may say,

"You got those for me!.......I mean.....you know I am not like that!"

And you can - in response - say, for example,

"I know, but I saw them and thought of you.....so I got them for you. You know how much I love roses!"

Don't be judgmental! Don't be saying,

"You know I love roses...but you won't get them for me....What *the hell* kind of a Man are you?"

Because this would totally *kill* his acceptance towards the whole *flowers* thing and you'd be, most definitely, judging him; therefore, you would not be ALLOWING him to be himself. I am sure there are many other things such a man would be doing in his ALLOWING state, which clearly indicates his *Love*.

And, as an aside, why would anyone require anyone else to conceptually "show them love" anyway? It's like saying, "I am *not* sure that you *Love me*; therefore, you must keep-on reminding me of how much you do or else I am likely to *fall out of Love* with you!" This is the prevailing, fear-based, directive in place in our society. It is precisely what subliminally forces men to be required to constantly "show" or "prove" their Love. Wanting someone to so call consciously "show love" is, once again, an "expectation" - we know all about expectations and where they lead. Love is about "a giving" (ALLOWING), and not an *expectation* of any kind! *Love* is *not* about "showing Love;" *Love* is about *being Loving*; and *being Loving,* is all about being accepting of others as they are. Being accepting of others, in turn, is the cornerstone of all *ALLOWING.*

As mentioned several times earlier, *Love* is about how much you're *ALLOWING* that other person to be themselves, to *Love* you *how* they *Love* you - without any added requirement from you to *show*, *prove*, or *do* any other specific thing to satisfy your Ego's demands. I know this is next to impossible for some of us to practice or even fathom, but that's simply how much that other person can *Love* you - period! They cannot *Love* you more.....or in any other way! Get that! *Please* allow this to sink in.

However, to get back to our example, if you continue to *ALLOW* him to just be *himself*, sooner or later, he may slowly be encouraged. Then one day, he may go-out and see some roses or a bouquet of flowers he thinks you'd like, and get them for you. And guess what? You eventually got what you wanted all along, by only placing your "expectations" unto yourself, and by *ALLOWING* him to just be. Therefore, in his *ALLOWING* state, and in his own time, he decides *on his own* and without any pressures or threats from you, to buy you roses. He obviously felt good and natural about doing it when he did (I think this should always be the ultimate goal: him truly *wanting* to do whatever he does, instead of doing "whatever" just to satisfy his woman's expectations!). No judgments on your part; you approached him with unconditional *Love*, which is completely interchangeable with *ALLOWING*. As long as you're able to make this your habitual way of being, *wants*, *expectations*, and all other *demands* - especially of him - become unnecessary. You'll now be on the road to *a truly blissful existence* in your marriage or relationship. It's the *only* way!

## The In Search of a Savior in Men Mentality

In addition to, and in many ways related to the above commonly-occurring views on life, the women in our society sometimes also seem to be relentlessly *In Search Of Saviors* in Men. This is a well-known phenomenon in common practice: Some women tend to vehemently believe - deep within themselves - that a man's duty is to somehow "save them;" this being their primary purpose for having or wanting men in their lives.

We can partially attribute the source of this type mind-set, to the fact that most religious organizations refer to God as being a *Man* ("God made man in his own image and likeness..."), and Jesus or Mohammad or whomever, as being "The Savior" or "The Messiah," etc. Since God is described as being omnipotent - all-powerful and all-invincible, among other things - it follows that it may seem *normal* or likely that "human" men *should* also possess some, if not all, of these very same traits and qualities, especially when they pertain to and is of some benefit to women. However, unlike God, the prevailing way of thinking is that "Worship," as in worshiping God or Jesus, etc, should never be expected *of him* (the particular man) from his woman, but *must* always be expected *from him* towards her.

"I'll just stay at home and wait until I find the *perfect* guy...or he finds me!" Some women would be working and taking-care of themselves, and it's almost as if it's an ongoing burden for them to be doing this. They would often openly make statements such as,

"I hope I can one day find a man who would take care of me....... someone who would "save me" from all the troubles and responsibilities of the World.....and give me the life I Deserve!"

We can also partially attribute this *In Search Of Saviors* in Men mindset to the whole Prince Charming, Fairy Tale, childhood-instilled, belief system in common practice today. Once again, the guy's sole purpose is to "save" the particular woman. As a direct consequence of this *expectation,* some women entirely dismiss their own inborn creativity, their own abilities for self-sufficiency in life. In some western cultures, for example, it's all too common for some to stay at home, patiently waiting to be discovered by *Men* who are willing to marry them or, more accurately, willing to "save them from themselves," in my opinion.

The paradox is, when the typical woman finds this alleged "Savior" and invariably recognizes that he's not exactly the "Savior" she fantasized him to be, all of her heightened *wants* and *expectations* are immediately shattered, leaving her even further *lost* and even more *puzzled* about life! Then, her thoughts are likely to take the form of,

"Something is wrong with this picture! Ok.....it's not me (Remember:

it's *never* her!); therefore, it *must* be him....he's is not the *right one* for me!"

And she, once again, goes in search of this "Savior" she believes to be out-there, somewhere, with her name stamped on him or, more precisely, with her name stamped on his *wallet* and on his *mind,* to conduct all his *living* and *dying* moments solely in an attempt to please her by meeting all of her needs and demands.

Even the women who are, so-called, "Achieved in Life," most times, still embrace this *In Search Of a Savior in Men* mentality. Have you ever wondered why loads of "highly-achieved women" are either *alone* or can't seem to *keep-it-together* in relationships or marriages? The proverbial mindset is usually one of,

"If I have "all this" already (on my own), what exactly *CAN A MAN DO FOR ME*......to validate the significance of his *presence* in my life?"

Don't get me wrong, this is not usually what they'll say out loud in words; but rather, it would be the 'operating air' or prevailing body-language given-off and ultimately picked-up by the men who typically only take-up *temporary residence* in their lives. The irony is, when the particular man, in question, happens to "have more" than the particular "highly-achieved woman," he immediately becomes the symbol of her *expected* "Savior Figure" once again (and not merely because he has it; he must also be spending it profusely on her). In the face of this, the added critical dimension due to her so-called "financial independence," immediately goes away.

Have you ever wondered why they say "*money problems* always lead to *break-ups* in marriages?" I would like to give you a personal assignment to find-out or discover for yourself (by whatever research method you choose to use) what gender usually "picks-up" and ultimately initiates these money-related "break-ups?" You may be lucky enough to discover something completely contrary to what I did. However, my own experience and research revealed that the common outcome follows the pattern of: No *money* = No *Savior* = I can no longer have you in my life, or it's time for *you* to be *REPLACED!*

As an example of this, let's turn our attention to my friend who got married *straight* out of college. Within 4 years, he had the two kids, the house, the home, the whole commonly-perceived picture of perfection. I once worked with him at an engineering firm in Florida, and I remembered, clearly, that he could not even go out for a drink with "The Boys" on Fridays; that was a *no-no* for him. He refused to go-out for a drink with "The Boys," because he thought or deeply-believed, he was doing the "right thing" by being and doing what's "expected of him," by society, his religion, and his wife. Big Mistake!

Anyway, at the time, I did see certain tell tale signs of possible pending problems brewing in his marriage; but, nonetheless, I decided not to interfere since I am of the opinion that individuals should be allowed to live and conduct their own lives in the way they see fit.

In the time since then, we've communicated back and forth - occasionally. Approximately 3 years ago, he told me he was about to get-into a real estate venture, but was somewhat disappointed due to the fact that his wife clearly indicated that she had no interest in being involved. When I asked why he thought she felt that way, he informed me that she shared no clear reasoning for her lack of desire to be involved, but made it clear that she simply didn't want to, for seemingly unknown reasons to him.

At the time, the real estate market was booming in America. His perceived venture was to purchase properties and hold-on to them for a few years, to allow their market-value to increase, before selling them at a supposed profit. In addition, he would also be putting renters into them, in the interim, to reduce or eliminate any possible financial burden to himself and his family. Personally, I thought it was an excellent idea, since I was also doing the same thing, on my own, in a completely different city and state. From an observer's standpoint, I saw the idea as being *good thing* for himself and his wife to work together towards a common goal as a family. So much for ideas!

Anyway, he *got-in* - on his own - and for some reason, his plans didn't exactly work-out as expected. The details go on and on. But, the point I want to make here is, you are a married couple, and *you're* hopefully trying to become self-sufficient as a family – and why not? In an attempt to achieve this, you would think the woman you marry would want to fully support you in this effort, since it would be ultimately beneficial to both of you when and if it works out. Now, you may have different dreams: you may want to get into *one thing*, whereas she may want to get into something quite different. However, the question becomes: What exactly does she have as a viable alternative for both of you to pursue? In other words, what is she suggesting as a workable possibility to make something "out of the box;" something out of the all too familiar "Rat Race;" or something out of the present Corporate America, *chasing their own tails*, BS? According to him, she communicated no ideas of her own; but, nevertheless, found it absolutely necessary to simply refuse to support his proposition.

I believe the one main purpose behind any cohabitating union, or relationship, or assumed life-long partnership of any kind, which includes the infamous *Institution of Marriage*, is for individuals to mutually provide support to and for each other - especially so in pursuing and realizing their dreams. The way I see it is, if his proposition would not be affecting or removing finances from the regular sustenance of the home, then why not support it? He may have in-sight into *something* viable that you are unable to readily see.

During all this, I was on the *side-line* watching it all unravel, and thinking to myself:

*I guess that's the way life goes sometimes. Is this really what marriage is all about: killing each other's dreams and aspirations?* Is it possible that her mindset may have been centered on the opinion of, "If I am "the victim" and he *should be* "my Savior," then it is *NOT* my *CONCERN* to be participating in *saving* myself – is it?" and this conviction only served to cloud her judgment?

With time, the "no support" thing became more and more puzzling to me; especially when I saw what he was going through in an attempt to make his dream for his family's financial future into a reality. By this time, he had already bought at least 3 or 4 duplexes. Between the effort of making the transactions, doing the cleaning, painting, and overall prep work to make them tenant-ready, along with the processing and qualifying of prospective tenants, preparing lease agreements, collecting rent, and still keeping and maintaining his regular, stress-filled, 9 to 5 Corporate America job, this guy had much more than his *hand-full* to contend with.

At the height of it all, since we're "good friends," I couldn't keep my lips *zipped-up* any longer!

"I don't quite understand all this!" I one day exclaimed - in disgust bewilderment. "How could you've made such a *BIG* mistake in choosing such a *selfish* woman to marry?" I further inquired. "You keep telling me exactly what's going on, and *it's a crying shame* your wife won't even lift a finger to help you! I'm sorry, but that seems *selfish* and *inconsiderate* to me!"

He never did reply; even though I could clearly see, from his facial expression, he understood the validity of what I was saying.

Personally, I hold such viewpoint because before I would ever *get-with* and even remotely fathom the thought of making a woman *a wife* (and I know there are lots of views on wives and husbands, and what they "should" and "should not" do and be), I need to *know* (and of course, I am also quite aware of the fact that there are no guarantees here either), comfortably in my mind, that this woman is "in my corner." I support her and she supports me – unconditionally. In other words, we mutually support each other, without the need for any semblance of persuasion, coercion, or *force* from either side. We do this because that's *exactly* what we individually want to do!

Often, the average woman doesn't seem to ever get-it, that the ultimate success or failure of her man (or husband) and therefore, the family as a whole, is largely dependent on the *level of support* she affords him in *all* his endeavors. I consider this outlook to be absolutely and unequivocally necessary in order for any marriage or life-long relationship to work. The following is applicable here as part of my interpretation of the symbolism concerning Adam and Eve in the Garden of Eden according to the King James version of the Bible: God originally passed down the *Law* to Adam; Eve chose to *break* it. Adam in-turn *followed* Eve (not Eve *followed* Adam), and *they both suffered* the consequences. Think real hard about this!

Also, in our society, women tend to always find it necessary to "buy-into" the latest trend or system-imposed gimmick - while *pulling* their men, *head-first*, into whatever it may be. This is the one reason why, I believe, Jim Jones of the infamous *Jonestown Massacre* in British Guyana in the late 1970's was able to pull-off what he did; the majority of victims being women and children. The women initially bought-into the gimmick; the children had no choice; the men, who had choice, blindly followed along; and the *inevitable disaster* followed, *as always*!

To this end, in the society we live in, it seems as if women generally gravitate towards being "Followers" (The in Search of a Savior Syndrome maybe?). Men, on the other hand - when rightfully poised - seem to be take-on natural Leadership roles. However, when a man has a woman in his life who does not *believe in him* enough to support him *as a Leader*, my advice is for him to not let it (the relationship) "blossom" or, more accurately, "wither" any further! Leave it alone; it can only get worse!

With time, my friend's situation only worsened – as expected! His wife began getting overbearingly restless, since, I guess, the "Savior" in him does not seem to be appearing soon enough for her; and of course, she still would not support him in any of his endeavors. In addition, as always, he's still home 'straight' from work just about every single night like clockwork. By now, the *mystery* between them is *long* gone! What *mystery*? There's absolutely no *mystery* left; yet, he continues to believe he is doing - and had always been doing - the "right thing" all along.

Don't get me wrong, I am not in any way blaming his wife for any of this; nor am I blaming him. Why would I? These type situations are designed to spark self-rediscovery, which prevailing circumstances tend to facilitate in many instances. As a Man, he *should* make it his business to know his rightful place. When I say, *know his rightful place*, I mean, he's supposed to know what it means to be *a Man;* and if *he does not,* then maybe he should be asking somebody, or seeking the advice of a married friend or acquaintance, who has his life together, is in obviously control of himself, and is able to maintain his own Power in his relationship. The key here is *you cannot be a Man for anyone else;* you *can only* be *a Man for yourself!* This necessitates reiteration. Once again: *you cannot be a Man for anyone else;* you *can only* be *a Man for yourself!* And in order to be *a Man* for yourself, you *must* know what it takes to be *one!* And it is absolutely *not* through living up to the usual judgment-oriented, externally-fabricated, identifiers and labels commonly used to tag men.

I used to often ask myself the following question: What's the best way to keep a woman? My answer to this question has always been, and continues to be, the same - every time! Whatever it takes, without instilling *fear* or using *force* of any kind, is the *only sensible path* to keeping a woman. A woman can whine and say, "I want *this*" or "I want *that*" or "I want *the other;*" but as *a Man,* you already know, by default, exactly how to act and what to do - even-though most men, through lifelong hereditary conditioning, *totally, totally, totally,* ignore or doubt this inherent *knowing.* Instead, they typically allow themselves to be pulled, pushed, and tugged - upwards, downwards, and sideways - while harboring thoughts of *worry and fear,* especially the *worry and fear of losing* their women, uppermost in their minds.

It is a proven fact that when a *Man* - any *Man* - allows his woman to corner him into submission, or to push him into a corner, to the point where his "every move" becomes predictably anticipated, that in *very short* duration, she will naturally and irreversibly *lose* all attraction for and towards him!

The title of this chapter: "What Should a Real Woman Want And Expect of Her Man," was primarily written for the sake of women; but nonetheless, even-though this was indeed my motive, I hope every man gets a chance to read and thoroughly understand and digest the underlying *gist* of what it is saying here. You see, the woman – referred to above – would no longer want to be with the particular guy, any longer, because he has become *totally uninteresting*, dull, and full of boredom to her! And as a result, *the mystery* between them (whether he wants to ignore it or not) died a natural, untimely, death! Why? Because he had been fitting himself into *an image*, a label, a subconscious identifier, if you will, that was subliminally passed-to and accepted by him as who he *should* be, and how he should act. Therefore, he had not been acting as his true, authentic *self*; rather, he had been acting on what's "expected" of him, based on what this same woman believes to be "right," based on what society says his role "should be," and ultimately, based on what some Religious persuasion dictates, typically. Understand that this approach does *NOT* work - and never did - because none of these forces really knows him or you!

*What works*, lies only within you! In order for you to *know* (not *believe*) what works, you've got to mentally reach *within* yourself and be willing to trust what's there. One effective way of achieving this, is through meditation. Meditation allows you to look beyond the physical you, and to become *one* with the true, *knowing* essence of your inner (spiritual) self - which most of us have long ignored, or have forgotten altogether. With this new found awareness, you'll no longer allow any *external*, organized or unorganized, fear-based, controlling, *System* to tell you how to *act* and *be*; you'll now finally understand the true meaning of what it is to have and to exercise "Freedom Of Choice" through unselfish respect and appreciation for yourself and all others: what it takes to be *a Man!*

In addition to all this, it's peculiar sometimes how much this same *Savior* figure (God) comes under *worldly scrutiny* by so many, when outcomes or situations occur in our *World of Form* that are not in-keeping with the *man-made* viewpoints of "How things *should* be" or "How things *should* pan-out," if God is indeed really in control; what God *should* and *should not* do and allow, in their opinions.

For example, after the incident in New York City on September, 11th 2001(referred to as 911), when terrorists allegedly *brought down* the World Trade Centers, many religious individuals in our society, began asking

WHAT SHOULD A REAL WOMAN WANT AND EXPECT OF HER MAN?

themselves varying versions of the question: "What kind of *A Savior* (God) would allow such gruesome events to take place?" In other words, they elected themselves as Judges of this very *Savior* (God) they would *normally* uplift and worship when things are going in what's perceived as "their favor" or "as expected" by them. They found it absolutely necessary to pass judgment as to what they believe *The Savior's* (God's) motives truly were in allowing such an event to take place. There is absolutely no question, in my mind, as to why the accepted and supported course of action in response to the 911 attacks was to take revenge, rather than learning the inherent lesson or lessons.

Again, there is almost always some manner of judgment directed towards this *Savior* (God) if the *expected outcome* is not what's anticipated of him. In our society, this *judgment* is commonly passed-down or shifted unto men at two distinct instances in the average long-term relationship or marriage. If it does not *show its face* in *the beginning*, it follows that it may *show its face* at the end - pretty much being the sole cause of it; and occasionally, in some isolated cases, it may be continually *showing its face* throughout the given relationship.

I have personally concluded, from my own life experiences and from those others have shared with me, that there is common practice in the beginning or courtship stage of relationships, for so-called "more mature women" (those between 30 - 35 yrs old and above) to display a "Where is my life going?" "I am in-search of *a Savior* to take me there..!" type demeanor. As an outward indication of this inner landscape, the average woman would meet a prospective male and, typically, she'll have-in-place a special list of conditions which he needs to meet in order to qualify or be disqualified as a man she wants to date. The main purpose and body of this list, centering mostly on her urgent inner dialogue of: "Is he going to be my *Savior*?" Or "Is he going to do *what I want him to do* and *be what I want him to be*?"

Driven by this all-too-common *fear-based* outlook, the average woman would have sets of questions that she will proceed to ask in specific ways.

*P "Nalagy" Browne*                                                                                     144

She would also be quite aware of the required responses, as to how or what his answers "should be" in order to allegedly "know" "if he would be willing to *be* and *do* whatever I want...so that I won't have to *waste* any more of *my time* with yet another man;" the usual principal focus of her externally-driven inner dialogue.

She'll then proceed to clandestinely ask these questions; and according to how he answers, he would be *judged* as being viable or not viable for her specific agenda. He would be *judged* under the criterion of "Should I move forward, or should I move-on?" "Is he worth my time and effort?" Or whatever else - Ridiculous!

Sometimes, you've got to be careful what you ask for; because you may get it, and chances are it may not be exactly what you really hope for or expect at all! Unknown to a large percentage of these type women, is the fact that there are *loads of men* out-there that are quite aware of this prevailing mentality among women. So when such men discern that women are going through their "lists" of pre-qualifying questions, they'll know exactly how to respond in order to be favored. The women get the qualifying answers they were looking for; and as a result, they'll blindly get into relationships with such men, solely based on the perception of getting all their "wants" and "expectations" allegedly fulfilled. There is profound truth to the saying, "The More You Look, the Less You'll See!"

As I alluded to earlier, this approach to life will *ALWAYS, ALWAYS* disappoint! Of course, the typical guy already concluded that if this woman is willing to do all this to "get a man or husband," to *be* and *do solely* what she wants and expects, then, chances are, she is a selfish, *Drama Queen*, with an endless storehouse of *Luggage* from past relationships. No *Real, Self-respecting Man* wants any of that in his life; he sees it as belonging on the curb awaiting pick-up!

I know some may say,

"No! She's just *simply* trying to protect herself!"

But the *real* question is: *From what?* What exactly would she be trying to protect herself from? *No one really knows - anything!* I know my last sentence sounds naïve to most, but *do you really know* if you're going to be able to finish reading this page? We're here, and we're all carried on this journey that I like to refer to as *The Dance of Life*; we're all subjected to the unavoidable *Law* which dictates that "Whatever type energy we *put out,* we shall simply *get-back*." My advice is to put out the *right* energy or message, *put out* the right signal; you'll surely *get-back* and experience whatever it is that matches *perfectly* with whatever you put out. If you keep-on putting out a message of *FEAR,* by harboring fearful thoughts about what you "don't want," you will indeed experience more than enough reasons to continue to be fearful. If you continually harbor thoughts of being *DECEIVED,* you will most definitely have such occurrence appearing *left, right, and center* in your life! You've got to understand that someone may *get with you,* for example, and, in their mind, they may be thinking,

"I don't really know if this is going to work-out." Or "I am not sure if this is the ideal person (woman) I want in my life...."

But guess what? Like I mentioned above, *No one really knows* the outcome! You may get involved, and things may shift. Then, before you know it, you and this person are *head over heels in-love* with each other. *STOP* allowing *FEAR* to destroy your possibilities! Don't think you know *ANYTHING!* Always keep an open mind about *EVERYTHING!* And above all, *LOVE yourself* – unconditionally (whatever the outcome); no one else can do that for you! Unlike popular opinion, loving yourself does not mean being fearful of life; being fearful of life indicates that you don't really know how to love yourself!

The more you come to understand, realize, and accept the fact that *you really, really don't know,* the more you'd be open for true guidance towards receiving what you really-really want in your life, and the better and more stress-free your life would be. Simply put: *God* (Supreme intelligence) *ALONE* controls *the outcomes!* You are *indeed* a part of *GOD;* therefore, when you truly trust-in and Love yourself - unconditionally (subduing your Ego), you'll naturally let-go of your need to control *outcomes;* you'll then come to realize that all of the *outcomes* in your life - in the past, the present, and the future - are *ALWAYS exactly* what they were and are divinely designed to be.

I know some are probably seeing this as crazy, wishful-thinking, on my part; however, if you choose to keep-on living your life forcefully trying to orchestrate *outcomes*, and by thinking and acting upon the premise of "I *must* have this *that way*," and "I *must* have that *this way*," you'll be - and probably are already - a very miserable and unhappy person! If its money you're after, for example, when you get the money, you'll become filled with the *FEAR* of trying to keep it safe, of trying hard not to lose it all. And then, guess what? What about the other areas of your life? You'll be living your life solely centered on *trying to keep your money*! That would be the complete focus of your life! "My life revolves around me trying to keep my money" would become your primary reason for living. This also directly applies to Love. Is there any *room for happiness* in this? Let go! Let go of *EVERYTHING!* Let it be! Not that you're going to be out-there "blindly walking;" but understand that you put your message out, and then you *ALLOW* what you intend for yourself to unravel in your life; simply *ALLOW IT!*

If you're a woman who's out-there researching guys by clandestinely asking men "willing to *do* or *die*" pre-qualifying questions and all such *nonsense*, on the premise of this being the only effective way of finding "exactly" what you think you "should" and "must" have, because it's absolutely necessary for you to be careful about what you're doing and saying, for example, you're putting-out a resounding message of *FEAR* into the Universe! As a result, you *can* only experience more *FEARFUL* occurrences in your life! We *always* get exactly what we're expecting, whether we're conscious of it or not. If this approach hasn't *worked* with all the other men you've dated, thus far, why exactly do you think it would *work* now or ever? I believe I just defined *insanity*?

Also, as a woman, you may think what a man *says* should be of utmost importance to you, since it clearly indicates all that needs to be said about him - as per the inculcated judgment of most. However, most times, this practice of prejudging men, through their words, can be extremely misleading. A man's greatest power, in the average woman's mind, is put into effect when he holds his words, when he has nothing to say about whatever! Why do you think women are always initiating divorce, or ending relationships, due to what they deem to be a "lack of communication" from their men? Some actually believe their man's words give them power; so when this seeming "power" is absent, they invariably become overly frustrated with the relationship; they have no tools to use to cast judgments on him.

In my own experience, I have met an endless array of women who all seem to incessantly cling to men's words. All his actions would be saying everything she needs to know, but for some reason, she *must* hear it said in words! And some would say, "I want words backed-up by action!" But, once again, there is *really* no *BACK-UP!* There is no *PROOF! STOP* looking for it! *ALLOW, ALLOW,* and *ALLOW!* It's the only way to have, be and experience, what you *REALLY, REALLY* want in your life. Stop fighting! Please let go!

The other perspective on this, is the "at the end judgment" of the supposed "Savior" as a direct result of "failed expectation(s)." To return to my friend's situation discussed earlier in this chapter, his wife seemingly had a *time-constraint* as to outcome – in place. In her mind, what she thought the "Savior" should be *to* and *for* her, was probably not happening soon enough; so recently, he told me she confronted him with the "I don't think this relationship is growing," and the "we're not growing together..." speech; as if to say, it was and has been "his duty" to conceptually make the relationship "grow."

In my mind, in situations like this, if the woman has a picture of "growth" in mind, how exactly is the relationship to "grow," in any way, if all she does is continually complain (typically) about her selfishly-driven, unmet expectations of him? And what exactly is "growth - anyway?" What signifies "growth" in a relationship? The mere idea of *forcing* what's commonly referred to as "growth," in any situation, is a ridiculous *expectation!* Can any one of us *force* or even apply any type of time-line to the *expected* rate of growth of *a tree*, for example? Definitely not! Therefore, how can we conceptually conceive it to be remotely feasible to apply this principle to any relationship? Only *Mother Nature* knows the answer to this. Leave it for *Nature* to decide. Life can become such a joy, when we finally begin understanding ourselves through observing nature. You *cannot control* the "growth" or outcome of anything - no matter how hard you may try! And please *STOP* with the *expectations* - especially of others. Allow things to naturally flow. Let things evolve - *NATURALLY*. Let them unravel at their *own*, God-given, pace. Leave it alone; it will *be* exactly what it's *supposed* to *be!* Has it ever occurred to you that if it does not work-out, then that just might be the way it *should* be?

So the *point of decision* or *the end* comes. My friend's wife, apparently, now judges him from the standpoint of him not doing what he was *supposed* to do in the marriage. As a consequence of this, all the blame for her continued frustration and discontentment is placed entirely on his shoulders. In other words, his *sole* life's purpose - in the marriage - was to make and keep on making her life significant, in her eyes. If he's not doing precisely that, then he must not be "The One" (The Savior) for her. Accordingly, she now wants a divorce!

"I have no responsibilities, but to just be here........because I am supposed to be *provided for*; I am supposed to be *made* and *kept* happy; I am supposed to be....." the entire exhaustive list! "He's supposed to make me "cum;" he's supposed to *this*; he's supposed to *that*; he's supposed to *EVERYTHING!* The only responsibility I have in this marriage to just *show-up!*"

Believe it or not, on the side of women, the preceding is the type mindset that is being relentlessly displayed and encouraged in our society. The main issue here is that the men don't seem to be *getting-it*; they don't seem to understand that all the negatives they continually face with respect to their women - all the seeming troubles, all the perceived puzzling thoughts, judgments, and the like - are all as a result of their own doing! If one were to make it their business to examine every organized society and culture throughout our inhabited world, one would unequivocally come to the realization that, in all cases, the women's general demeanor or behavior towards their men, remains a direct by-product of what is allowed to *fester* by these very men. America is the *Melting Pot* of just about every possible race and culture throughout the world; therefore, if one were to closely observe the practices and relationship interactions between the men and women from other parts of the globe, one would become fully aware of the truth to this reality.

### Seeing Their Men as the Proverbial Science Project

Remember when you were a kid in school your teacher would often give the class an assignment to do a *Science Project?* Usually, to proceed with your given project, you often first received the project description laid-out on a task sheet. You were then to proceed to gather all the necessary materials you need and go to work. The one important thing about the typical *Science Project* is, in most cases, you were directed to record the results you obtained, and are to compare these results to previously-established outcomes. This will enable you to conclude if the procedure you ensued was accurate or successful.

Here, we can take the entire above process and apply it to the general mentality of the women in our society when it comes to the men in their lives – especially so, those they call "husbands!" For the most part, women typically see their men, conceptually, as "Science Projects." As it follows, if the desired outcome of the particular "Project" (the man) does not pan-out in a particular way and in the particular time-frame, as expected, then to her: "Something *must* be wrong with the procedure I followed!" "Something *must* be wrong with me." Or "Something *must* be wrong with him!" More commonly, though, most don't *ever* think anything is *ever wrong* with them, per se: their ridiculous expectations; their overall mentality and views on the roles men "should" and "should not" play in relationships, etc. And therefore, the men usually end up bearing the blame for the perceived *failure*; a process which they themselves, nine times out of ten, knew absolutely nothing about!

As it stands, the women more often than not see their men as *Projects*; these things they *must* "work on" for a specified period of time to mold them into what they think they *should* be *to* and *for* them. I know most men have heard their women say – some time or another – something to the effect of: "I've wasted my time with you!" In other words, this is equivalent to the particular woman saying, "I've wasted my time working on you (the *Project*); so now, I am moving-on to a new *Project* to see if I get the expected results or *outcome* I was looking for!"

Essentially, this type would seek-out and marry prospective men (choosing the particular Project). Immediately after marriage, they would begin displaying the "need to proceed with my project" attitude. I don't know why, but some would conclude that, "It's just in a woman's nature to act and be this way." In my mind, the only truth to this, rests in the fact that it's simply what she has adapted and accepted as being her reality; what she "should" do and how she "should" be and act.

However, most would begin acting on the typical mindset of, "I *must* change him into what I want him to be" instilled by either *Tradition*, or through some type of mental picturing planted earlier into their subconscious, as to what they *should* want their husbands to be like – for them!

I recently interviewed a woman, who just got divorced again for the 2nd time from the same man. During our conversation, I commented on the fact that it seemed obvious to me that a strong bond does exist between them, and that they should've probably tried a little harder to work things out. She immediately became overly defensive,

"This is not the person I want in my life! I have the picture of whom and what I want in my mind, and he is definitely not it!"

I continued to explain to her that according to my understanding of what she was saying, the picture of this person she has in mind, for herself, must be in-keeping with herself as well - as she really is - being careful that she also fits into that same picture. In other words, she cannot be expecting perfection in the man, while she continues to see herself as being faultless; she must see and accept where she too has her own short-comings. As long as she's able to grasp and clearly come to grips with this reality, she'll then probably reconsider, and may even want to remarry the same guy for the 3rd time; this time, for the long haul.

However, I soon realized that, in spite of everything I shared, this woman *still* expected all sorts of other insurances, securities, and the like from men - the typical woman, from my experience.

Women often deduce that it's their God-given *right* to expect guarantees from men! It's amazing how common this expectation actually is. Most never grasp that life itself has no such assurances. As a wise woman once wrote,

"Security (itself) is mostly an *illusion!*"

I cited an example earlier in this chapter concerning a woman who dated a particular man for approximately three years, followed by another three years of marriage, who filed for divorce on the grounds of him not being her "Intellectual Equal." I openly laughed at this when I initially heard of it; I considered all of it to be outright hilarious! Nonetheless, if we examine the *big picture* of what really "went-down" in actuality, all it's saying to us is that this particular "Science Project" did not turn-out the way the woman expected it to; therefore, she had to abort her involvement with the failed *Project,* and simply move-on!

If you're a woman who dated a man for all those years, you *know* *exactly* what he's like all along – no questions about it! You're either going to accept him for who he is or you're not! The peculiar thing about all this is, after the woman told me her girlfriend's predicament, I eagerly awaited her comments on the issue. She had nothing further to say! Instead, she started rambling-on about something quite different. I stopped her 'dead' in her tracks!

"Wait a minute.....you see that as being ok?" I exclaimed.

"I don't know.....I guess she expected him to eventually *come-around*....."

She passively replied, as if surprised and puzzled by my question.

"Are you listening to yourself? I continued. "So I guess because he married her, there's some kind of supernatural thing that *should* take place to somehow *change him* into exactly *what she wants* him to be; and if this transformation does not take place within the given time-frame, then it *should* be ok for her to just replace him, right?"

There was no further reply....

When I realized that the woman saw the actions of her friend as ok and agreeable, needless to say, I was flabbergasted! It then struck me that this very mindset must really be an epidemic in our society! I do agree that individuals should be *free* to do whatever they want to do in every situation *(Freedom of Choice)*. However, when someone finds it necessary to cast judgment on another, based on their *expectations* of that person fitting into their perceived "Science Project" out-come, they're setting themselves up for inevitable failure, and, at the same time, they'll be adversely affecting the other person's life with their ignorance! Your purpose *here*, in this life, is to *be of service* to others. That is the sole purpose of each and every one of us! You should always be true to yourself; but at the same time, you've got to clearly understand that other individuals *must* be allowed to be true to themselves, also! This is especially necessary in a relationship or marriage setting if it is to be remotely workable to any degree.

The following is what *being of service* to others means to me: Total acceptance of others - without judgments; while giving of your self, wholly and unselfishly. A relationship is *never* all about you! As explained earlier, *ALLOWING* is the key here.

I'll continue a bit further here by adding yet another dimension to this; one that I briefly touched on earlier. When the desired *outcome* of the perceived "Science Project" turns out to be *exactly* what's expected of it, something rather strange frequently happens....Strange! It's almost equivalent to someone finally owning their dream car, for example. Initially, they'll start out embracing the novelty and excitement of merely acquiring it. Then in short duration, it soon becomes as unimportant to

WHAT SHOULD A REAL WOMAN WANT AND EXPECT OF HER MAN?

them as an old, broken-down, piece of furniture; it loses all its glory.

Some women would fight and fight to presumably get or secure the outcome they believe they *must* have with respect to the men in their lives, all in an effort to *change* them into whatever they desire them to be! Nevertheless - and this may even surprise you – it is very common to see that the more and harder the particular woman fights for this change or "Science Project" outcome that she conceptually thinks she *must* have, the least she will typically appreciate the *change* if and when it comes!

Don't get me wrong, I am a firm believer in freedom, that no one should be desiring or forcing anyone else to be or do what they want or expect them to be or do; however, I have concluded that there are some women who ceaselessly display a "never being satisfied" persona in the eyes of their men! Meaning that, no matter what you are or do, as a man, they're never-ever pleased or satisfied; it's simply never enough! Whether deliberate or otherwise, it remains the prevailing perception upheld by the majority of men in our society today. And that's the reason why I always advise men to remain steadfast in whoever they are. And to every woman I date, I always encourage to Love me for *who* I am - as I am, because I *only* love and appreciate them for *who* they are - as they are.

I remember some time ago, in response to my commenting that "A woman has got to love me for *who* I am," a male friend exclaimed...

"But, wouldn't you be trying to change her?"

"How exactly would I be trying to change her?" I retorted.

"You would be trying to change her into wanting something other than what she wants!" He continued.

"How exactly would I be trying to change her into wanting something other than what she wants? I snapped! "I am who I am! The fact that she wants to change me has nothing to do with her changing herself! If she wants to change, then she should put all her efforts into trying to accomplish just that. Are you actually suggesting that I *should,* instead, somehow change myself to fit into what she wants me to be?"

"Maybe.. Isn't that what every woman wants?" He added, now with a calm, inquiring, tone.

"That's crazy! This might be a tell-tale sign of why your relationships never last, guy; you keep forcing yourself to change into a new person – every time: the one you believe every new girlfriend wants you to be! Stop chasing your tail, guy! Sooner or later it gets stale, and you'll surely be left disappointed, confused, and frustrated with yourself. Been there, done that; and most importantly, learned from it!" I concluded.

He left the conversation with a whole lot to think about!

However, in practice, there's a flip-side to all this. In my own experience, and from the experiences other men have shared with me, some women have this same gripe with the men in their relationships seemingly attempting to "change" them. Just about every guy I've discussed this issue with, somehow sees the complaint as being entirely unfounded, however. To this end, I'll share a related experience I had with an ex-girlfriend, while we were engaged in a high-energy discussion on politics:

"Why are you trying to change me into thinking the way you do?" She accused!

Totally thrown *off-track* by her perplexing accusation, I was like

"No.....I am just having a discussion with you.....it's about me; my personal views and opinions - it's not about you! We're simply having a discussion! And I am not trying to tell you how to think; I am just sharing with you how I think! That's all! If you think differently - that's *fine*.......I am most definitely not trying to change you into thinking the way I do!"

To this very end, I've been in situations where I'd be involved in a discussion with a woman (usually someone I happen to be dating at the time) and she'll sometimes make an accusation to the effect of,

"...You're only taking the opposing position, because of the stance that I am taking.....aren't you?"

This allegation says a few things to me. First, I asked myself: "What could possibly lead her to think that I would deliberately do such a thing?" To conclude that I would - by default - be internally slated to play *Devil's Advocate* by intentionally taking the opposing position to hers is quite beyond me! Secondly, if I had said words to that effect, sometime in the past, then I could clearly understand her making such a comment at a later date, in reference. However, if that never transpired - and it hadn't - why exactly would she be thinking that I would want to oppose her? Unless, in her mind, she believes her sole purpose should be to oppose me; and therefore, expects the same of me towards her! Hence, by agreeing with me - for whatever reason - she would be somehow showing *weakness,* and would conceptually be "giving-in" - so to speak! I believe we may be on to something!

Often, this is the type thought process women in our society have bought into, embraced, and identified with as their own; and so, come out here dishing-it-out to men every single day! Relationships are not meant to be battle grounds! No one has to *win* or *lose!* Sadly, most men just accept this dogma as simply "the way it is" and correspondingly try their best to deal with it.

For myself, I will always remain steadfast in who I am. In that, my acceptance of a woman is *never* going to be a change of me - *now or ever!* I am who I am; I love and appreciate myself, *as I am;* and I am capable of loving and appreciating whoever the particular woman may be, *as she is -* as long as my loving of her does not demand or require any *forced change* to myself. Ironically, every man I've known, who has allowed forced change upon himself to fit-into his woman's obvious ego-demands or "Science Project" outcome, it has invariably turned-out to be a negative for him and the entire relationship, as a whole. Always!

In conclusion, I want to reiterate here that as far as the question goes: "What Should a *REAL* Woman Want and Expect of Her Man?" I strongly believe practicing and adhering-to a continual state of *ALLOWING* is probably the one most effective way of being that will afford the relationship or marriage a fighting chance to weather the inevitable storms of this life, and ultimately, to provide it with the necessary tools needed to withstand the test of time. I am convinced that *everything* in an effectively-working relationship, all rests on the crucial importance of practicing *ALLOWING* on either side. And at the cost of repeating myself: As long as you're able to make this (*ALLOWING*) your habitual way of being, *wants, expectations,* and all other *demands* – especially of him – go straight through the window! You'll now be on the road to *a truly blissful existence* in your marriage or relationship. It's the *only* way!

# CHAPTER 8

# What Should a REAL Man Want and Expect of His Woman?

Here again, I strongly recommend that "a *REAL* Man Should Want and Expect." absolutely nothing "of His Woman" either! The same applies: the same *ALLOWING* is of extreme importance for men to practice, also. And of course, the idea of seeing and observing the true essence of their women, which is also identical to their own true essence, as in seeing themselves in their women – spiritually, is also very important to practice and adhere to. This approach will serve to enable men, as it did women, to stop the *judging,* and to simply accept their women in their "own skin," as they are. Again, this approach is probably the only course of action to follow in order to truly and unconditionally feel and *ALLOW* the emotion we call *Love* to flourish.

Be that as it may, in common practice, things take-on a relatively different landscape with respect to how men interact with and towards the women in their lives. Often, a number of issues lie in the fact that, typically, men are raised to believe their sole purpose is to somehow "fit-into" or "live-up-to" the preconceived picture *they believe* women hold of them; a self-view most have grown to accept through parental *misguidance,* cultural codes, etc. In other words, as men, they tend to evaluate themselves from the standpoint of doing a kind-of self-judgment type thing to see, for example, "How well do I measure-up to the "expectations" of this woman?" I've concluded, through research, that there are two main underlying drivers behind this self-defeating approach taken-on by a considerable number of men in our society.

First and utmost, the majority is so preoccupied with competing with and *sizing-up* other men for the attention and approval of women, that, without effort, most unknowingly *ALLOW* their women to simply continue to be who they are, which can definitely be a good thing, depending on the underlying motive or reasoning behind it all. In any event, this *ALLOWING* approach is commendable; it's always *a good thing* to *ALLOW* others to simply be themselves. However, in this case, the men's passive reasoning behind this act of *ALLOWING* has often created added negatives; both among themselves, and in the way their women correspondingly act towards them.

The seeming unending competition between men for women's attention and approval has been a major contributor in preventing any noteworthy platform for male-to-male bonding in our society. This is especially evident in areas concerning not only with gaining a better understanding of their women – in general, but has also contributed majorly towards deterring males from being more supportive of other males when personal relationship issues arise. The latter definitely not being the case among women!

Then we have the resulting negatives surrounding women and the way they interact with their men. Due to the fact that, for example, women are commonly *ALLOWED* to simply be themselves from the onset of relationships, this has translated into the typical woman commonly believing that she is somehow "perfect" – and especially so in the eyes of the typical male. This male-encouraged, misleading, self-view, only serves to by-and-large "wake-up" the proverbial, ever-present, Ego in the average woman. Often, instead of her, in-turn, also practice *ALLOWING* him to simply be himself, as a consequence of him catering to her from the onset - sending a message of "You are faultless in my eyes," mostly to gain her attention "over the other guy" - in her mind, this catering or "treatment" *must* continue *even* into areas which include "changing him" to further *fit-into* the picture she holds of herself; the one that was typically instilled, subconsciously adhered to, and fully supported all the way from childhood.

Remember one thing: once you start feeding the *Ego*, it will always want *MORE*; it cannot *comprehend* what it means to ever be satisfied; it's all in favor of wanting *MORE of* and *from* others! This "feeding" of the woman's Ego, leaves the average man in a state of "giving-up" his endowed *male essence* or role, for a *LIFETIME* (in the case of marriages)of attempting to "fit-into" a life image which matches his woman's mental picturing of how he "should" act and be towards her. Talk about *losing yourself?*

The paradox is, once he gives-up his true "male essence"( and he usually does) by continuing to play and adhere to the role (or roles) the particular woman expects of him instead of remaining *truthful* to who he really is, it soon becomes absolutely necessary for her to start demanding more and more changes out of him. This is simply how the *Ego* works!

In a short time (after a few years, usually), the man would have totally and unknowingly bought-into and, pretty much, have now become the "Improvement Project" or "Pet-In-Training," which the typical woman has to "work-on," more and more, to further turn into *EXACTLY* what she believes she wants him to be! It never ends!

This is the point where true turmoil usually sets-in, if, and only if, the particular man were to begin resisting any of the further changes demanded of him; the onset of which marks the point where he characteristically begins showing signs of his pent-up frustration with the pretenses; "The Charade" he thought was only supposed to be temporary in the beginning! *Good Luck!*

Secondly, in men, there's an all-too-common inner compulsion or "life-line urgency" for *being of significance* to the particular woman in their life. "I must be of significance to this woman.....no matter what it takes....this is what I need to be and do to gain and maintain her undivided respect and attention!" This seems to be the typical inner directive upheld by such men.

To live-up to this self-appointed, Ego-driven, fear-based, image some men would rob, steal, kill, and do absolutely *whatever* it takes! The local and state prisons in your particular country or state usually house a significant number of inmates who fits precisely into this criterion as the unfortunate reasoning behind their incarcerations. Some would kill; whereas others *have killed* their entire families – including themselves – all driven by an untimely incident such as the loss of a job, which, in their minds, represents a threat to this inner compulsion for *being of significance*! "Since I can't be the Provider that I *must* be, then I am compelled to do the next best thing: take the lives of *all* parties involved!" This compulsion has proven to be THAT serious for some.

Often, men would try their endeavor best to fit into this "one thing" they believe to be so-so very important to women; however, to some women, this assessment of them may not be at all accurate. Let me provide you here with a personal example, concerning a woman I once dated.

Very soon after we  initially met and started hanging-out together, a number of her male acquaintances individually pulled me aside and clandestinely informed me of how much "She is all about money...." and whatever else. My response, at the time, always took the form of a non-verbal nod, and an internal "Ok, let's see if there's any truth to this." Yet we dated exclusively for approximately three years or so, and not once did I ever hear or see any evidence to substantiate their conclusions about this woman! As a matter of fact, it was the complete opposite: She wanted to spend *loads of money* on me!

What I've realized from the experience – among others – is that there is a large percentage of men in our society, who deems it necessary to approach women with their, so-called, "Needing to be of significance" demeanor; and so, they'll start spending lots of money on a woman in the beginning, for example. Then later-on, they'll want to somehow change this platform, with the thinking that it "should" be now ok and acceptable to her! They've already begun the *game plan*; and now, they want to suddenly make a change in the middle of the *game,* the one they volunteered to initiate in the first place - not realizing that what ever platform they came on, they'll very likely have to stay on!

I know some would label such a woman as a "Gold Digger;" however, I beg to differ! If he volunteered to start the process, he becomes the "Gold

Giver;" she never "Dug" for anything, he volunteered to give it freely! If you approach the typical women flaunting money, and later *you have none*, how do you expect her to stay with you? Always think insightfully about the long-term effects of what you're about to create before beginning the creation process.

Conversely, if, as a man, you approach a woman speaking "truth," "life," and "value," and that's all you're about; then guess what? You have more "staying power" than with the *money!* Remember this: The "money" is the "what" that you are; the "truth," "life," and "value," are the "who" that you are! The "what" is likely to change; the "who" never changes!

A friend once told me that every time his wife emphatically says to him: "I don't understand you!" Or "I can't seem to ever *put a handle* on you!" He says he goes out to the local Bar and he celebrates; he drinks a beer or two to commemorate the momentous occasion! According to him, when his wife makes such declarations, it's a clear indication that "The relationship is going *very* well!" Now I am not saying I've bought into this mindset as to be representing the truth; but, obviously, he has his reasons for adhering to such a principle.

However, one day I ventured to ask him to explain the reasoning behind such a puzzling viewpoint. What he said blew me away! He explained that

"The more a woman understands you, the more her mind wanders..... the least she understands you, the least her mind wanders. She's going to always be trying to understand you; however, the day she does is the day the mystery goes! So, not that you're trying to puzzle or confuse her, but when she says those words, it simply means you're not "pegged" as yet! Once you're pegged – look-out!"

I took his advice and pondered on it for a while. For about two long weeks, I couldn't think of anything else but this unusual concept this guy shared with me. Then I began reflecting on my own life: Since childhood, I've always been an individual who strongly believes in just being me without having to put-up pretenses about anything. I try not to be selfish, or disregard the woman in my life; but, by the same token, I am always going to be myself in every possible way. Here, we are examining the premise, "What Should a *Real* Man Want and Expect of His Woman?" and I guess, as men, we can look at this and see it as probably being something that merits consideration. Is it at-all possible that his concept could be accurate? I still wonder about that.

To go further, some men tend to see their women as what I refer to as "Moms." They see a Mother in a Woman! They identify with a woman, as someone who *should* clean-up after them; clean their homes or living space; cook their food; etc. They seem to *simply* want to replace "A Mom" with a wife or woman!

Initially, my first inclination on this was to assert that *I don't agree with such a view of women;* however, I have learned that people are going to be what they want to be. If my woman feels as if she wants to do something for me - she can; if I feel as if I want to do that same thing for myself or for her – I will; and vice versa. I have no *expectations* of her - whoever she may be. I place no "You're supposed-to(s)" on any woman! Instead, I prefer to allow *freedom of choice*, without expectations or judgments from me. This is just my personal perspective on things.

As mentioned above, there are far too many cases in our society where the men view their women as literal *Maids!* The women are supposed to cook; they're supposed to wash; they're supposed to clean, and perform just about every other domestic chore for them. Traditionally, women often buy-into this expectation of themselves as being normal. Many Latin and other European cultures such as the Italians, for example, have been culturally slated to be this way for endless numbers of generations. The women would say, for example,

"If I have a man - especially a husband...I know I am supposed to (XYZ)."

In many such cultures, only girls are reared to do house work. The boys typically grow-up expecting this service from their mothers and sisters; whereas the girls, in-turn, grow-up with the expectation unto themselves to provide this service for the men in their lives.

# WHAT SHOULD A REAL MAN WANT AND EXPECT OF HIS WOMAN?

I think such an outlook puts unwarranted burden on women and on relationships, as a whole! Of course, if the particular woman really wants to do it, then I guess it would always be her choice to do so. However, when performing such services becomes an obligation, it typically takes-away from the whole spontaneity of the relationship. In my mind, we as humans operate best when we feel completely fulfilled while doing whatever we're doing for others. Because of the fact that an "obligation" is always connected to an "expectation" and vice versa, this association literally blocks the ability for any feelings of fulfillment on either side of the spectrum. How? Because the "obligation" is always conducted specifically to fulfill or live-up-to an external "expectation" of someone else; and by the same token, the "expectation" always rests on someone else to fulfill a duty or chore that supposedly *should* or would satisfy the person having the "expectation" of them (an "obligation")!

Remember: All feelings of being fulfilled, including Love, only come from you! In other words, nothing outside of you - be it an "expectation" or an "obligation" - can provide you with any sustained feelings of personal fulfillment. Feelings of being unfulfilled, always lead to disharmony and discord in relationships. These are commonly displayed in the form of guilt, blame, bitterness, enmity, discontentment, and ultimately, verbal and physical abuse in many cases.

This situation brings to mind a very close friend, who, since High School, has lived with one girl after another – back to back to back – without ever taking a single break. In a nutshell, it's as if he believes it to be virtually impossible to, temporarily or otherwise, operate on his own. According to him, he *needs* to always be living with a woman, because he *must have* someone to cook, clean, and do his laundry, etc.

In addition, he *must* also be sleeping next to a woman every night! I know some would probably conclude: "Well, he's just being a Man.... what is wrong with that?" Nonetheless, this can be the tell-tale signs of an unhealthy dependency or *attachment* or worse. This state of dependency, can cause individuals - especially evident in men - to not only *lose control* of their own emotions, if and when things don't work out in their favor, but, in addition, some are also apt to commit outlandish crimes against the very same 'objects' of the particular *attachment* or *obsession*. Why? Because their actions would then be directly driven by the same *obsessive, eternal, attachment*; at which time, typically viewed, only within the confines of their own twisted minds, as being justifiable for what they'll erroneously refer to as "deeply loving and not wanting to live without that other person!"

On a lighter note, we can, for example, equate this process to someone frequenting the Clubs every night – *directly* from work and even on weekends; never-ever getting an opportunity to spend any significant amount of their waking time with themselves. In short duration, they're apt to become *addicted* to being on the streets and in the Clubs. Soon, they'll get to a point where they'll feel entirely lost and out-of-place if this *addiction* or compulsion were to be abruptly changed or removed from their life.

Understand that you *cannot* truly enjoy yourself with anyone else, *until* you're able to thoroughly enjoy yourself with yourself! You *must* make it your business to become very comfortable with conducting yourself on your own! Really make it your primary concern to get to know yourself! Put simply – no one can find *you* for *you*!

I do know some may say, "It's a good thing that you (he) can't conduct yourself (himself) on your (his) own.....we all 'need' somebody!" This foolish notion remains the primary self-view at work in our society. Far too many of us have bought-into this idea of *dependency* on others as being a commendable *way of life*; erroneously calling it *Love* – until, of course, we're on the receiving end of a stalker, an obsessed individual, or worse!

It's most definitely not "a good thing," because a person who can *stand alone* is the person you want as the backbone or *figure of strength* in your life! Unlike popular belief, being able to *stand alone* is not being selfish; it's the complete opposite. Also understand that if your so-called *Love* is based on *dependency*, it can never be real *Love*! It would be exactly what I just mentioned – *dependency*! And *dependency* - like *Fear* and *Hate* - is the total opposite of *Love*; it only exists through weakness! *Love* is about *Strength*!

*Love* is about *Power!* Never *Weakness!*

Dr. David R. Hawkins describes it perfectly in his powerful, ground-breaking, book: "Power VS Force." On the sentiment of *Dependency,* as it relates to what our society deems to be *Love,* he wrote:

"...When frustrated, this emotion (what we typically refer to as *Love*) often reveals an underlying anger and dependency that it had masked. That *Love* can turn to *Hate* is a common perception, but here, an addictive sentimentality is likely what's being spoken about, rather than *Love;* there probably never was actual *Love* in such a relationship, for *Hate* stems from *Pride*, not *Love.*"

Make it your business to get to know and appreciate yourself - thoroughly!

## What Men Appreciate Most About Women

On an even lighter note, but - nonetheless - well in-keeping with the premise of this chapter, I will now examine two commonly-occurring personality or character traits, possessed and displayed by a significant number of women in our society; their importance here centering on the fact that most - if not all - men find them to be absolutely irresistible!

For this discussion, I will go out 'on a limb' here and assert that just about *every man* has an almost uncontrollable attraction for any woman who displays *a girlish-type demeanor,* or *a girlish-type innocence* about herself; this being typically coupled with an added, equally attractive, *passively independent* demeanor. Meaning that, the particular woman could be grown, for example, but nonetheless, there still remains something girlishly-sweet about her personality. Not the *girlish-type innocence* one would mistakenly refer to as being "Dumb" or "Uninformed" or "Ditsy;" but, there is an all-encompassing magnetic web which she unconsciously weaves about herself that just about every man gets caught-up-in when in her presence. Let's take a closer look at this *girlish*-type *innocence* phenomenon.

The "girlish-type innocence" phenomenon is something we as men collectively refer to as a woman being "extremely sexy," or a woman having or possessing "exceptional sex-appeal." Of course, since nothing in life is absolute, there are times when one may go beyond this outer display, and venture to further meet and start communicating with such a woman, and come to find out that their initial instinctive perception was wrong or misleading. It happens!

However, for the most part, women who display this attractive *girlish innocence* about them are indeed the ones men just simply *lose their minds* over! Often, this trait is so-so powerful that, physically, the particular woman may not be typically what we as men would normally "go crazy over;" however, in spite of this, the *girlish innocence* she possesses somehow transcends all this, and manages to still give her an irresistible, "Out Of This World" type sex-appeal to most men.

Often, the particular woman may seem to be all about *fun;* she is almost always in jovial, happy-go-lucky, lighthearted, easygoing spirits; but, don't be fooled! As a result of her overall enduring demeanor, she always seems to be able to keep her "cool" in crises situations. This, in-turn, invariably brings an unmistakable "everything is going to be alright" calm to the particular state of affairs, whatever they may be – every time!

Also, her inner ability to always maintain even composure in crises, serves to reduce stress and anxiety in others, and, at the same time, allowably promotes the ability - in others and in herself, as well - to explore viable solutions to aid in rectifying the particular existing calamity, rather than remaining stuck on the prevailing "what is" of the situation.

Further, without question, I am indeed convinced that these are the type women "Real Men" crave to have in their lives! They typically want to share life with this type, and simply because such women are able to generate renewed vigor, renewed spirit, and overall feelings of inner rebirth - coupled with visions of unlimited life possibilities - within them. That's right: The woman a man chooses to spend his life, time, and space with, *can* and *will* unquestionably affect his possibilities in life; and especially so, in the way of his happiness, his success, and his overall life achievements! Did I miss anything?

All too often, though, we wonder why older men sometimes seek-out, date, and even want to marry, younger, more *girlish-type* women. Personally, I believe most – if not all – women did possess and displayed this attractive *girlish innocence* trait, to some degree or another, at a younger age, but for whatever reason – consciously or subconsciously – chose to abandon it later-on in life. There are others, though, who through passively subconscious, or actively conscious effort, are able to continually embrace and display it throughout their lives. For the latter, it seems as if this trait remained a naturally-occurring part of their God-given make-up for life.

In any event, these are the women who are usually very happy! Why? They simply *ALLOW* their men to keep-on being themselves. They don't appear to *take-on* the usual 'heavy,' hard-pressed, auras about themselves. They don't appear to *take-on* the typical demanding demeanors, as in the "I Deserve(s)," the "You Should Know(s)," and all the other related "Drama-Bearing" attitudes; the ones most men vehemently prefer not to have to deal with!

Instead, these women cling to an unmistakable - almost childish - girlish way of being that, as I mentioned earlier, every 'single' man, in every 'single' society, and in every 'single' culture - when I proceed to discuss what I mean, and they come to realize exactly what I am referencing - all agree: it is indeed the resounding truth! It actually comes across as if there is something natural-occurring in the psyche of all men that uncontrollably attracts them to this energy.

I must go a bit further here, and call attention to the fact that even those men who were previously diagnosed as being afflicted with sexually-related troubles (and the following is especially well-known among men), may sooner or later encounter these *girlish* type women –younger or otherwise – and suddenly, "out-of-the-blue," start feeling as though they were 18 years old again! Often, the situation would unfold as a direct result of getting caught-up in the all too familiar "positive energy cloud" given-off by these women. In other words, the men would typically start experiencing all the exuberance and vigor of their teenage years, seemingly at their finger tips, once again. And as a result, "everything" (and I do mean *EVERYTHING*) typically returns to their normal functionality! Were these men *troubles* physical or age related; or were they solely psychological? - A question to mull over.

Also try to understand that this positive energy is by no means possessed or given-off by the younger girlish women only! As I alluded to earlier, there are "older" women, possibly in the same age group as the typical "older" man, who somehow manage to still maintain their *girlish innocence* characteristics in full swing. I guess we can safely conclude that the supposed *"change"* or abandonment of the trait is not necessarily something a woman decides upon voluntarily; and most times, it may be the outcome of a conscious decision, based on something to the effect of:

"Ok! I am older now; I need to start making demands...... time is *running-out!*"

And all such nonsense! Then the particular woman correspondingly abandons her God-given nature, and soon picks-up or replaces it with the *hard-pressed*, Ego-driven, "I've got to get mine from him....since he *owes* it to me" attitudes described above.

Nonetheless, for the women who are able to maintain this *girlish innocence* attractive energy about themselves later into adulthood, it is not essentially so because they somehow remained naïve or immature or inexperienced, in any way; most do have what we view as "regular lives" with *good*, productive, careers going - like everyone else. But there's just this enduring, wonderful 'thing' they continue to possess and embrace throughout their lives: When they go places, doors always open for them. They incessantly get 'passes' coming at them - 'left' and 'right' - wherever they go. In many cases, some even experience much younger men getting all-caught-up in this energy they exude; and as a result, would often be making relentless effort to "get with them." This energy is *indeed* irresistibly attractive to the vast majority of men – regardless of age!

Then, we have the *Passively Independent* disposition, which typically comes along with the *girlish innocence trait*, just discussed. When both traits exist together, and are equally displayed by any woman, to men, this transforms her into the absolute "cream of the crop" among all women! Again, this is the type woman just about *every man* wants to share life with! Let's dig deeper into what makes this so?

First, this woman has the *girlish innocence*, which is the attraction: irresistible, undeniable, sex-appeal, etc; and this, more often than not, keeps deepening with time. Second - in addition - she has the *Passive Independence* trait going. This means that she's fully capable of taking care of herself – financially; she's doing very well in her own career, making "good money" and the like; but - and here goes the *punch-line* - she does not feel or act as if the money she makes, suddenly transforms her into "An Independent Woman" with respect to her man! And she does not believe, for example, if she happens to bring home a *BIGGER* paycheck than her man or husband, that this qualifies her to take-on an "I wear the pants" type attitude, which would correspondingly make him feel as if he is "less than a man!" She *empowers* him in every way, rather than *breaks* him *down* in any way!

It seems apparent to me that this type woman can and will be an incredible symbol of support in any man's life! That is exactly what she typically is: She has the independence with which most women would take and see themselves as "I don't *need* a man;" and she's able to use it, and instead, truly understands and conveys the message that she *does need* her man - just like her man *needs* her! And not actually "need," as in "I must have or else I'm going-to die" type "need," but she shows him "You are here in my life, and I want you to know that I appreciate you, and want you to be here with every fiber of my being!" This is what her actions would be saying without any words needing to be said.

When the average man is accustomed to being with the type woman who acts as though (and most times, she may not even be remotely "Independent" in any way!) she must "Demand" something by virtue of being a woman: "I am *this*..!" "I am *that*..!" "Hey, you *better do this*.... or you *better do that*... etc," he would invariably welcome the above positive, refreshing, change with wide-open arms! I know I would!

The average woman does not seem to understand how constant complaining and other perceived negative demanding attitudes literally "kill" her man's attraction towards her! In a word, they eventually make her "ugly" to him! Often, she could be, physically, the prettiest, most appealing "looking" woman in the world; yet to her man, she may *not be* "this" anymore - especially if she's the type that continually complains about what seems like "everything" to him!

My own experience and research, have brought me to the realization that men are like this: If a woman keeps-on using the act of sex against them, for example; they must act and be a certain way, or else they don't get "this" or they don't get "that" when they make advances - which always come across as undue, senseless, punishment to them - sooner or later, they're likely to become completely turned-off; losing all desire for the same woman they once deeply and uncontrollably yearned-for!

Unfortunately, this process materializes far too often in our society. It is to a woman's advantage to recognize that all men dislike *complaining*. If they are continually subjected to it - unchecked - they'll eventually start disliking the *COMPLAINER!* You can actually dislike someone you *Love*; and especially so, if they incessantly refuse to *ALLOW* you to simply be yourself!

Unfortunately, this is the usual point where men - especially married men - claim to have been forcibly 'pushed' to start seeing other women; those who, temporarily or otherwise, show them how much they're accepted and appreciated - just as they are!

I know some may probably be thinking, "Well, women can do the same too…" And to this, I will ask the questions: Would that be the appropriate solution? Do you really think the answer rests in conforming to the practice of *tit-for-tat*, instead of stepping back and coming to terms with the true cause of what's transpiring?

I think the answer lies in individuals moving to a place of learning to appreciate each other for *exactly* who they are; and in relinquishing *all judgments* – otherwise (*ALLOWING* – discussed in detail in Chapter 7). This means, unconditional *acceptance* on both sides. It is a well established fact that any form of punishment - or any version of it - inflicted on anyone else, for any act or failure to act, on any level, and for any perceived selfish or conceptually unselfish gratification, irrespective of the other person's opinion, viewpoint, or value-system, constitutes the outcome of an inner *judgment*. *Judgments* and their resulting *punishments*, when practiced in relationships, only create undue pressures, which violently eats-away at intimacy like a raging case of cancer in the human body; they render the functionality of the relationship *inoperable* in every possible way!

Anyway, even though I would never claim to have all the answers, I do know this *one thing* for sure: that the women who adhere-to and continue to display their *girlish innocence*, coupled with being *passively independent*, described above, are indeed the most desirable women on the planet! I would further suggest that, should the typical hard-pressed, complaining type woman (you know who you are) desire to cash-in on the insight provided here, she may want to make it her business to try and emulate at least some of the qualities of the *girlish innocence-passively independent* type woman described here. Of course, this may prove to be a challenge for some, but at least, they'll know, with certainty, what it is that men desire and appreciate most in women.

Once again, every 'single' man wants this type woman - whether he knows it or not! It is the one thing, I believe, every *Real Man* should passively "Want" and allowably "Expect" of the woman he chooses to share his life, time, and space with - if, and only if, he honestly knows what's *good* for him.

# Concluding Thoughts

For those who got it, I hope this Book was able to achieve its goal, in providing some level of encouragement, all in an effort to alleviate what I deem to be the main obstructions which frequently impedes mutual fulfillment in relationships and marriages. Whether one sees the viewpoints, ideas, and supposed solutions discussed within the foregoing Chapters as valid or not, can probably be attributed to perception; some of us may be ready for answers, some may not!

I have come to the realization that the fundamental *Answer to Life* is essentially *A Question - A Question* of Choice. Choice, I believe, is everything! This Choice, although typically manifesting itself, sooner or later, into the physical acts which positively or negatively affect our life's experiences, is invariably driven by the thoughts we choose to entertain and encourage; this being further directed, by our own personal self-view, or our overall perception of life itself. Our perception is in-turn influenced by the social and cultural *conditioning* we have been subjected to, and correspondingly uphold, from childhood up-until this very moment. Therefore, it follows that when we really look deep into the trenches of our lives, the *only* Choice becomes our *ability* – or our lack of recognition of it – to relinquish, or to continue to uphold, the many coats of *conditioning* our minds and, therefore, our entire consciousness have been clothed and contaminated with thus far.

This *ability* is *always* available to us; simply by virtue of us *being alive* – right here, right now! The problem is most of us are completely unaware of the immensity of our ability, and the fact that we really do *always* have Choice! So instead, the majority have voluntarily surrendered their psyche to an existence of self-imposed servitude, characterized by assumed lacks and supposed limitations. On a subconscious level, our abilities are *only* limited by what we *choose* to believe – period! Thus, our thoughts, which indirectly programs our subconscious mind, based on what we choose to process as "*Truth,*" is where I believe the focus for any positive change or adjustment needs to be. As author James Allen masterfully puts it in his book, *As a Man Thinketh*:

*"Thought and character are one; and as character can only manifest and discover itself through environment and circumstance, the outer conditions of a person's life will always be found to be harmoniously related to his inner state..."*

It is all about our level of awareness of what this "*Truth*" really is that supports and directs our perception of life itself. The more aligned our awareness is with this "*Truth,*" the more harmonious and fulfilling our life's experiences would be and vice versa. Your *conditioning* may tell you, for example, that sadness and turmoil is *normal* in relationships and marriages; you are to just expect it! It may even tell you that after a few years, "It's *normal* for married couples to *fall out of love.*" If you make the "Choice" to believe any of these so-called "*Truths,*" you are indeed doomed to have them manifest themselves in your life; after-all, they would be directly in-keeping with what you have *chosen to believe* to be *true* and *normal*.

Wherever such dogma exists, individuals are typically left scrambling to figure-out what is deemed supposed *Truth,* as opposed to what is deemed supposed *False,* and, in a word, *lost* in their efforts to find answers *out-there – somewhere*; even-though, in reality, all the answers they could ever want already exist *within* them. I know I have beaten this viewpoint *to a pulp* throughout this book, but I consider it to be of immeasurable importance for this one "*Truth*" to be known and adhered-to, if we are to move to any level of harmony in this life; it is that important!

Furthermore, throughout this book, every relationship issue outlined, discussed, or referenced directly relates to the affected individual's prevailing level of awareness to the foregoing simple "*Truth.*" Since every aspect of our functioning lives directly interrelates in some ways or another, the acceptance of "sadness and turmoil," as being *normal* and *expected* in relationships and marriages, for instance, often stems from the ingrained *religious persuasion,* which dictates that one *cannot* - and should not - trust and depend on oneself for answers. Why? Because, in doing so, one would be excluding God from one's life! In other words, the conscious act of trusting and depending on one's own inner, Universally-instilled (God-instilled), guidance system would, in essence, be rendering one as to be supposedly *"going against* God's divine will." This viewpoint really *does* make a whole lot of sense, doesn't it?

Then the situation is further amplified by the concept of rules, man's supposed sinful nature, punishment, and the like - further moving him away from self-trust and self-reliance. This added dimension is what I deem to be "The Final Straw!" Why? Because, ultimately, it is precisely what drives individuals to become hopelessly dependent onto others (Attached) for what we erroneously refer to as "love" and "happiness" - to say the least! *Something or someone out-there - somewhere - is responsible for the Love and happiness that I am supposed to feel for and within myself!*

As a direct consequence of this "Final Straw," we commonly find ourselves desperately clinging to a fear-driven, socio-economic system of demands and externally-imposed pressures, which is further characterized by an endless plethora of rules and regulations, sin and punishment, judgment and retribution; and to an existence of continually *attempting to provide* and *expecting to receive,* guarantees to and from others. Remember, it is divinely *wrong* for one to trust oneself, therefore, this trust *must* be found in someone else!

I want to make a timely distinction here, which happens to be in direct accordance with my own personal viewpoint and experience: *God is for us; never-ever against us! Again: God is for us; never-ever against us! God does not punish us; we punish ourselves, as a direct consequence of the 'bad' Choices we keep making. These 'bad' Choices, themselves, being made on the grounds of us allowing our Lower or Ego-Selves, which is the "in-the-world" view( or worldly conditioning) of ourselves, to direct our lives, instead of allowing our Upper or God-Selves to do the directing.*

*Also, the Source we refer to as God is pure, unadulterated, Love, Peace, and*

*Harmony. This Love is the ultimate organizing principle of the Universe; hence, the term, God! All that we seem to take for granted - every day (our breaths and our heartbeats, for example) - are all part of this ultimate organizing principle at work. Love and Fear are on directly opposing ends of this spectrum to Harmony (one's total awareness of this Love) like the North Pole is to the South Pole of the Earth. Just as it is impossible for one to physically exist at both Poles simultaneously, Love (Harmony) and Fear (Disharmony) cannot exist together. Therefore, Fear only exists in the absence of or, more precisely, in the self-negation of this Love, which is the ever-present, enduring, God-force existing within each and every one of us. When in any state of Fear, you are ignoring or negating this integral God-force-direction (Love), which is the only naturally-unchanging part of your and my existence. In my mind, this is the only REAL I know!*

I believe the answer is for us to begin viewing ourselves from the standpoint of what we truly are: complete, self-sustaining, beings - guided by the awareness of our own internal, universally-instilled oneness with omnipotence and omniscience. This new, truth-driven, self-view will then serve to radically improve our overall relationship to life itself, as we know it, and ultimately, improve our relationships between each other; and simply because, the customary, seeming necessary, practice of *Attaching* ourselves to things and other people, under the false premise of *Love* and *Fear of Loss*, for example, would be now rendered senseless!

*Our World of Attachments* is a *BIG-BIG* one! As a matter of fact, *"The Final Straw,"* mentioned above, as well as every other life and relationship concern I know – including, but not limited to, those discussed within the foregoing pages of this book – all manifest themselves through some level of *Attachment*; the *Attachment*, in-itself, being the final controlling step contributing to man's prevailing religious, socio-economic, and all other behavioral *conditioning*; and remains the culprit directly responsible for all known - past and present - global disharmony: war, hate, corruption, iniquity, and the like.

We seem to compulsively *attach* ourselves to life, to our possessions, to other people, to our reputations, etc. In other words, we tend to fervently *attach* ourselves to every aspect of this fast-passing *World*, not ever seeming to grasp the truth that we really-really-really *cannot* own anything or anyone! All we can do is temporarily use things, and enjoy and appreciate ourselves and others – including all of *their* and *our* own differences. There's absolutely nothing and no one to be owned - no matter how tenaciously we may desire to *eternally* cling to *(Attach to)* it or them!

Further, as Dr. Wayne Dyer once wrote: "All that composes - decomposes.." This includes the bodies that you and I presently occupy and everything and everyone else - everywhere - for as far as our eyes can see or our thoughts can fathom. In other words, *attaching* ourselves to anything or anyone, in this life, is crazy!

According to the world's most renowned spiritual teachings, we are all here in these bodies to learn necessary spiritual lessons (Unfortunately, the present system we live under - religious, social, economic, and otherwise - either has no clue, or does not see any benefit in encouraging or promoting this). After our bodies inevitably die, we either move-on to learn other spiritual lessons, or we return to the *Oneness from whence we came*. "*You*" - the energy that is "*You*" - can never die! Again: "*You*" - the energy that is "*You*" - can never die! And simply because, "*You*" are not the body; "*You*" are the animating energy of *Spirit,* which temporarily occupies and animates your body during this small fraction of time we refer to as your life. Know this! Sit quietly and allow yourself to become fully aware of this simple, but profound, truth! The sooner you're able to detach yourself from this outer *World*, the sooner you'll be able to start enjoying and appreciating every single moment of your life - including everyone and everything in it. As the popular, but widely ignored, Sufi saying goes: "You're in this world, but you're not of it."

I shall one day soon write extensively on the up-coming issue; but, for now, I will conclude here with a simple suggestion that I *know* would radically change the existing level of awareness and, ultimately, life itself in our present World and Planet– for the better. I am suggesting that we consider telling our kids, as early as humanly possible, that the name we give him or her, is the name for their physical self, but that they them self - the internal, animating, intangible spirit or life-energy of their unique existence - is *Love* itself. As an example, the following can be told to the young child:

"Honey, your name is John or Joanna, (while touching his or her body), but *You* (while touching or pointing towards his or her heart) are *Love*.... and here, you are the same as everyone else!"

This simple act, I believe, will completely change or finally reveal, the ever-present, but mostly overlooked, universal *Love* dynamics of our existence. It will achieve this by directly orchestrating, with time, a *Paradigm Shift* in worldwide awareness, starting with the *least-conditioned* among us: kids. The benefit here is the undeniable fact that this is indeed the entire *Truth!*

I am absolutely convinced that my suggestion here - if executed correctly - will eventually take our civilization to a level of awareness where we'll finally *get-it* that *Love* is not like the towel we pass from hand to hand, from individual to individual, from place to place, and from thing to thing - until it gets soiled, dirty, or useless; after which, we typically toss it out or replace it with a new or better one. In other words, you don't give *Love* and take *Love* away; you don't start *Love* and stop *Love*; you don't pass *Love* around and take it back if this thing you refer to as *your Love* is not being reciprocated in the ways in which you expect it to; and most profoundly, you don't have *Love* and not have *Love* - you are *Love* itself! The energy that wakes you up every morning; the energy that takes you through the day - everyday; the energy you use to think with; the energy that put's you to sleep at night; the energy that continually beats your heart; etc – is all *Love*. Therefore, once again, *You* are *Love* itself!

For example, thinking "you have Love" as opposed to "you are Love," creates two distinctly different feelings within the individual. Thinking from the standpoint of you *having Love*, fabricates the notion that this *Love* has to be acquired or obtained from somewhere outside of you. In addition, if "you have Love," then this means that you can also "not have Love," or you are likely to lose the *Love* you managed to acquire. This viewpoint alone, I believe, is the underlying culprit creating the all-too-common *Fear of loss of Love* outlook we see manifesting and perpetuating in our present society and World every single day! Stop right now, turn-on your radio or television, and listen keenly for the overwhelming evidence of this truth. It's *EVERYWHERE!*

However, when you start thinking from the standpoint of "you are Love," everything literally changes: you instantly start seeing the obvious truth of what (the ignorance) you've been buying into all your life; immediately, the whole futile idea of *having* or *not having Love,* gets transcended, the blindfolds are finally removed; and you now *know,* for sure, that you are already all the *Love* you could possibly need and want – right here, right now! In my mind, this universal understanding is exactly what's needed to *bridge-open* the door to all awareness.

The difference between God and you, is that God is the *Love* that you are, but don't recognize that you are. This has been the main contributor to the prevailing self-view of being separate from God. And here is where the distinction or validity comes in: Because God and *Love* is the same thing and God is everywhere; if God is indeed omnipresent, and God is, without question, *Love* itself, then this means the Love that God is also exists within you! If you cannot be separate from God, then you cannot be separate from *Love.*

As I alluded to above, it is not that you don't know you are *Love*; the fact is, you have consciously forgotten through the self-crippling worldly conditioning you have bought-into since childhood. So now, the answer is to stop the process *"dead* in its tracks," by releasing the hold the ego has on you in order to resuscitate the full awareness of who you really are! The objective here is to get us back to where we need to be, by focusing our efforts first on the kids, our most precious future commodity; the ones who are not yet as conditioned with personalities, egos, and acquired prejudices and biases, etc - the typical blindfolds and obscurers of who we really are. Once we can get this engine restarted with the truth, even though it may take a generation or two to materialize, life and this World will eventually take-on renewed value and meaning.

Can you foresee the mass positive possibilities such a simple act would eventually bring about in our society and World? Can you imagine: true harmony in relationships and marriages; no more need for divorce - as self-love would prevail; the elimination of all possibilities of war and iniquity among people; a zero crime rate; no more need for our present level of law *enforcement*; governments and businesses operating for the sole purpose of benefiting all, instead of for benefiting only a few; presidents honestly representing the people, rather than leading countries into Wars under the blindfold of ignorance and patriotism; etc? For those of you who possess true vision, it should immediately become crystal clear to you, that through this almost effortless act of awareness, all this and so much more can one day become our reality.

Imagine a world where kids would now see themselves in other kids; clearly accepting the truth that every person has the same value as every other person - everywhere! Imagine how far this would go on a global scale; we'll be actually fostering an entire generation that would serve to completely change the social and economic landscape of our entire planet. Can you see the clear truth to this?

Often, many of us like to loosely claim, "The Children are Our Future." I personally think there is multifaceted value to this statement of reality. For example, when we examine the layman's perspective on it, the kids are indeed the *younger ones* who'll one day be the *grown-ups* of tomorrow. This is where it begins and ends!

Nonetheless, if we are to take a more conceptual or philosophical view of this truth, we can see yet another dimension to it all. That is, *Responsibility* on the side of the present adults; those who happen to be aware, on the deepest level, of what this *Truth* really means; those who happen to be quite conscious of the prevailing flaws in the overall *self-view* in our present society and World - passed-down and adhered to for far too many generations; and those who are able to literally see these common generational follies from a realistic standpoint of *cause* and *effect*; thus, clearly understanding the indispensable urgency of what is suggested here.

To reiterate: If we are to teach our kids that they are indeed *Love* itself, then our kids would quickly realize that " Ok, this is my name…however, I am *Love* also…..That is his name or her name, but he or she is also *Love*." With this inherently-divine self-view awareness, an entire generation is destined to recognize, from very early childhood, that the *Love* in which they are - not by choice, but by default of their existence - is indeed *Universal*! In other words, the new generation's prevailing mindset will be now centered on, "This *Love* that I am is the same *Love* that every other person is." Bingo! Let's examine a few of the potential ramifications of this.

First, individuals would readily discontinue seeing *Love* as any form of *Attachment* to others. Since they'll now *know* that *Love* is something they are already, this *knowing* will permit the individual to finally feel centered and complete in his or her *Love*. By the same token, because this state of personal inner harmony fosters the discernment to see and accept the other person in the particular relationship as also being centered and complete in their *Love* (who they really are at the core), both individuals, as a result, would now effortlessly appreciate each other's uniqueness; and so, can actually be *One* in *Love* (what we falsely believe the act of marriage would miraculously bring about), without *ever* resorting to any desire or need to control, change, or otherwise possess each other (The typical results of the *Attachment* phenomenon).

Secondly, we can even move from personal relationships, and venture into the potential ramifications in business. Businessmen would now – not because one individual may be the Boss and the other may be an employee – respect themselves, within themselves; and by doing so, self-respect and appreciation for all would be encouraged and implemented across the board - irrespective of the previous (often set-in-stone) corporate-based hierarchical boundaries. A job position would be now simply seen as one's functionality within a particular company, rather than one's identity or personal importance, through the all-too-common *Status Labeling* in present corporate business practices today. In other words, every position, in every company, would be now viewed as being just as valuable as every other position - with absolutely no need or desire for exceptions!

Thirdly, we can go a bit further by anticipating its future effects on governmental bodies throughout the world. This would, in essence, be a direct by-product of its inevitable, impending global effect within and among people of different countries. On a global scale, individuals' internal dialogue with themselves would now hover around some version of the following: "Ok....I was born in *this* country. Another person may have been born in another country. My name is *This*, and I am from here; his name is *That*, and he's from there. He is *Love*....and so am I! Our names may be different; our cultures too may be different; but we are both fundamentally the same; what exactly do we need to be fighting against each other for? There is absolutely nothing to fight for. He is exactly the same as I am; I can clearly see myself in him!" This would be the milestone which marks the end of all wars and global turmoil!

I know the preceding concept may prove to be rather difficult for most to fathom - much less, accept as being truth or even being remotely possible; nonetheless, until we start seeing ourselves in others – from the person next to us on the highway, to the person across the other end of the globe – man's self-annihilation remains inevitable! There is much benefit to seeing and understanding oneself in and through others - not because you may not speak the same language or eat the same foods; the idea is to see beyond what your eyes see.

On a personal note, I could never grasp what the problem is? For me, people who look different than I do; speak in a different way or language; act in a different way; have different mannerisms; do things in a differently; etc – are all very intriguing in my eyes! It has always been this way for me, ever since childhood. From a spectator's standpoint, I've always embraced differences in views, life, dress, etc, rather than ever considering any other person who happens to embrace a different culture than I do as being foreign to or opposed to mine. To experience one person taking something to mean *one thing*, and yet another taking it to mean *something quite different*, is totally awesome to me!

However, of course, in our practicing world, what we have are *cultural codes* in place, which says: "You sound funny!" "You dress funny!" "You're strange!" "How could you possibly do things *that* way?" "You need to change!" "You have an accent!" And so on. Instead of continually trying to force things to be what we've grown and conditioned to see them as, my suggestion is for us to accept, allow, and embrace the universal *singularity* which remains inherent in the *multiplicity* of all things (also includes people)? This is what our Universe is really all about. This is what all of life is about. It encompasses the concept of God or Universal Supreme Intelligence itself: *The Singularity in the Multiplicity of Gods, People, Things, Etc.* It is the one concept that *must* become deeply embedded into our psyche, if we are to move from where we presently are; we need to entirely embrace it; we need to become *One* with it; after-all, it's exactly what we live and experience every, single, day. Spiritually, we already *know* the profound truth to this; why not simply accept it for what it is? Once again, the answer lies in our awareness of *Truth!*

*The Singularity In The Multiplicity of Things,* stems from the awareness of the constancy of *Duality* in our Universe and World; and becomes clearer, when we begin seeing all levels of *Duality,* as in tall or short; beautiful or ugly; black or white; up or down; etc - from a perspective of *Oneness.* Meaning that, for example, a person is only seen as *tall,* when they are compared to a person that is considered to be *short,* and vice versa. The *Truth* is a person is neither *tall* nor *short* or *beautiful* nor *ugly;* they are simply the unique perfection of their creation: they just are! Once we are able to see and embrace seeming *Duality* from a perspective of *Oneness* perfection, we will then voluntarily let go of all duality-related labels and codes of conditioning; we'll then fully grasp the inherent value in uniqueness.

To *paraphrase Thomas S. Kuhn, who first coined the term "Paradigm Shift" in his book, The Structure of Scientific Revolutions,* published in 1962: A *Paradigm Shift* is an overall change from one way of thinking to another; awareness being the indispensable prerequisite to all seeming acceptable change. In other words, as mentioned earlier, one must first become aware in order to be able to see the existing problem(s), issue(s), or needed change(s), from both sides (*cause* and *effect*) - for what they really are. Remember: This *World of Form* is a World of *effects* only! It is only in the face of this awareness, through spirit, that one will be afforded the ability to isolate true *cause*. It is only after true *cause* is identified and correspondingly changed, that any prevailing *effect* can be altered towards a more harmonious outcome.

We cannot expect to experience sustained harmony in our relationships, if we have bought-into, and continue to accept as normal, a system characterized by mass collective disharmony! Sooner *than* later, these discordant elements are bound to crop-up in our lives; we know the stories all too well! I see it as being equivalent to practicing unhealthy eating habits, while expecting to remain healthy.

There is a picture I like to paint for friends and associates, when they would often become confused and overwhelmed with life and relationship issues. It goes something like this: *If you were to buy a bag of assorted balloons and fill them (one-by-one) with water until they all eventually break, and somehow proceed to observe the aftermath of the actual balloons (what's left), you'll invariably discover that every balloon breaks in a different place.* In other words, what we think may be the results of a multitude of *causes*, may-very-well-be a single, but unidentified, *cause* manifesting itself into a host of different outcomes or *effects*. Overfilling the balloons with water, did cause each one to eventually break, however, chances are, no two balloons would *ever* break in exactly the same place.

To apply the this *truth* to relationships and marriages: I am convinced that the one *cause* which keeps manifesting itself into an endless assortment of diverse *effects* is the mistaken perception of supposed absence of, or the subconscious negation of, or lack of awareness of, the ever-present, pure energy of spirit, *Love;* the same unchanging *Love* that you and I are already by virtue of being alive – here and now! If you are completely unaware of or literally in denial of "what" you really are, how can you expect to ever "live" it? No one else can realize this *truth* for you! As The Bible clearly indicates in Corinthians: Chapter 13, Verse 13:

"…..Faith, Hope, and Love (Charity)

These three; but the greatest of these is Love (Charity)."

This *Love* is not something anyone is destined to give to you; it is what you are already by virtue of your creation! Know this, and you will immediately begin to appreciate what *Unconditional Love* really feels like!

THE END!

# ABOUT THE AUTHOR

The author's background puts him in a unique position to write this book. Born in the Eastern Caribbean island of Antigua, Patrick grew-up partially between New York City and the confines of the island's beautiful sunny shores, which he left after his immediate family decided to *pick-up* and leave for New York in the 1980's.

After graduating from Aviation school in New York City, Patrick worked in the aviation industry for a few years before moving to South Florida where he attended and gained his BSEE degree from The Florida Atlantic University in Boca Raton, Florida. He now resides in South Florida.

Even though he has always been fascinated with and personally involved in the Literary and Performing Arts, Patrick decided to go the *Exact Science* route (Bachelor of Science in Electrical Engineering) in college, mainly as a result of the many issues he had faced earlier in his life with the typical Literary Arts teacher or college course professor, who seems to think he or she *must always be right* - even though the particular course material may explicitly involve abstract subject matter that, by definition, remains open to personal interpretation.

Frankly, he has been often labeled as being "different" from the norm. He somehow managed to gain this label as a result of the fact that he almost never held the same viewpoints on *life* and *things* as the majority.....and for the most part still doesn't. This outlook – according to him – is not one he chooses to deliberately take to *get* or *spark* attention, as some might judge. Rather, he sees it as an inner, somewhat *self-direction-finding* mechanism, or "knowing," which he believes affords him the ability to process certain so-called 'realities' in life from an entirely different, fundamentally analytical, *cause* and *effect* type perspective. It's what he now sees as a gift from *The Devine*, or from *The Supreme Intelligent Source* of all, or, simply put, from

God.

Endowed with this naturally-occurring outlook on life, Patrick began honing his writing skills at a very young age. To this end, he has personally written many pieces of poetry, lyrics to songs, and an array of other literary pieces - all centering on insightful and more harmonious possibilities to life as we know it. At times, he would suddenly jump out of bed, in the middle of the night, and start writing '*a piece*' "often delivered to me in my sleep" as he puts it.

In addition, although his avocation has always been centered mostly on writing, there was always an added inner gravitational passion, which propelled him towards the pursuit of a deeper, more profound, understanding of life and truth. To this end, he managed to attract and immersed himself in the many works of such spiritually-directed authors as Carlos Castaneda, Dr. Wayne W. Dyer, Dr. David R. Hawkins, Ram Dass, Louise Hay, Khalil Gibran, and Deepak Chopra – just to name a few. This exposure to the many lessons, insights, practices, proven research, and spiritually-driven lifestyles of these authors served to further deepen the understanding he has of his *true-self*; and in doing so, also helped to expand his own insight into all of life to unfathomable depths.

Nevertheless, even though the foregoing has always been his prevailing inner direction, he used to consider himself to be a little weird in a self-conscious kind of way. So, for a long-long time, much of his works and views were never shared with anyone else. It was not until approximately two years ago, after writing a preliminary piece (which was to develop into a full-fledged chapter in this Book), which he asked two colleagues to review for their supposed differing opinions, that he got the feedback and overwhelmingly encouraging motivation bringing him to the undeniable realization that writing has indeed always been his true 'calling' in life. And not just merely to write, but to write with the unquestionable intention to impart insightful ideas and possible solutions based on "truth-to-life," and driven by a passionate desire for being of service to all.

Patrick fervently adheres to the principle that, *a different view, on a given subject, does not necessarily negate the existing view or views; but, most times, allows for a deeper, more profound depth and understanding of the particular subject matter in question.*

This, he believes, is what the underlying process of life, self-growth, and the awareness of unchanging *Truth* and wisdom are all about.

From 2001 – 2009, Patrick also held the position of Vice President and part owner of MVT Recordings, Inc., a record label which operated out of South Florida. In addition to his administrative duties, he also scouted for talent, and produced and co-produced a number of songs – both from a lyrical and a musical perspective.

Under the alias of "Nalagy," he presently hosts two internet- based radio talk shows: *The Pluto-Nalagy Show* and *The Inside-Out of Men – Uncensored*. These shows are weekly occurrences, both centered on a different and compelling relationship topic each week. The former discusses relationship issues and concerns from the very same perspective outlined and explored in *this Book*. The latter is a support forum for men to express and seek possible resolution to the many everyday challenges they typically face in our society.

9 780578 062853